HALF LIFE

CAMOUFLAGE

DAD'S DEAD

ROOM SERVICE

careful

Hypnomart

PERPETUAL MOTION
in the Land of Milk and Honey

3 ways to go

Love is all

Cowboys

JUKEBOX

SCRUTINY

LONDON
15th FEBRUARY
8

ANATOMY OF MELANCHOLY

Miles from Anywhere

rabbit

animate!

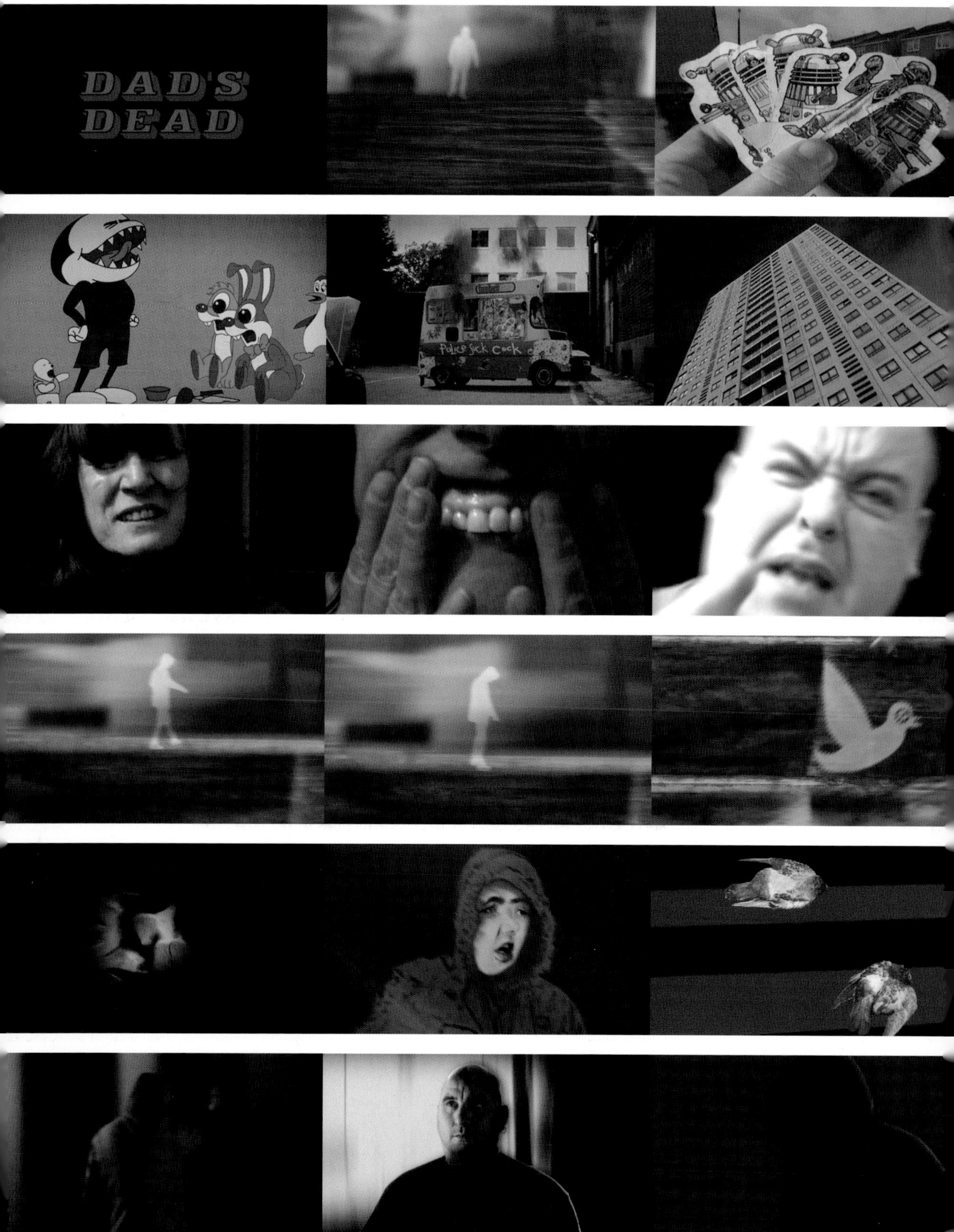
DAD'S
DEAD
Police suck cock

Dad's Dead Chris Shepherd (2002)/3

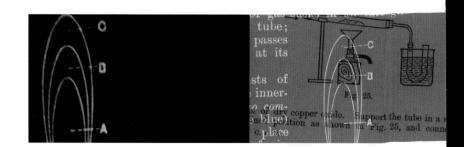

Contents

Edited by Benjamin Cook and Gary Thomas

Published by LUX, London
in association with Arts Council England

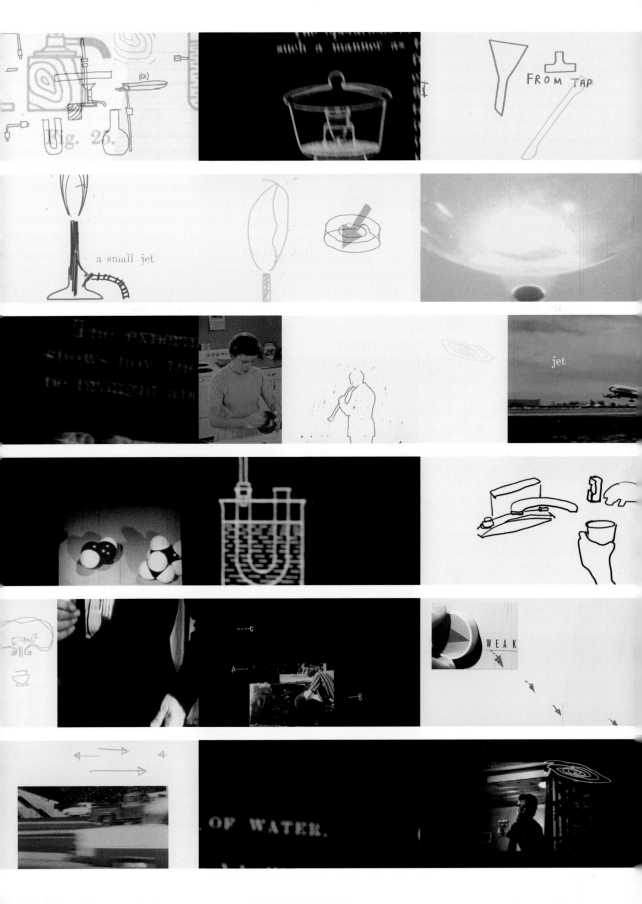

SCRUTINY

ORN

John Halas an

Scrutiny Ian Cross (1995)/7

Introduction/*animate!: the New Animation*

animate! was founded by Arts Council England and Channel 4 to commission groundbreaking animation works for television. A unique collaboration between public arts funder and national broadcaster, animate! has offered artists and animators a space to create work since 1990. The imperatives of broadcaster and arts funding are often distinct, but the ambitions for animate! are mutual: to offer commissions that are both opportunity and challenge for creativity and innovation in animation, and to get this work to a wide audience through television and beyond. animate! has commissioned 84 films to date, works which, taken together, represent the extraordinary breadth and diversity of contemporary animation. These works reflect a wide range of practice, tracking developments in technology, formal interests and artistic concerns, always posing the question 'what is animation?' with every work offering up a different response.

This book isn't the definitive guide to the animate! project but rather an exploration of the broad landscape in which the project is located, a place where art and animation meet and the 'possibilities in the moving image, way beyond live-action and the frame-by-frame confines of conventional animation,'(1) are found.

Animation production and practice has been transformed over animate!'s lifetime. In *Build It and They Will Come*, Gareth Evans and Dick Arnall track some of the key moments reflected in works produced through animate!

animate! has always sought to attract a broad range of practitioners, from artists wishing to realise ambitious works to industry animators taking time-out for personal projects. Mike Sperlinger's interviews with

animate!-makers illustrates this diversity of background, motivation and the very conceptualisation of animation itself.

Angela Kingston's gallery show *The Animators* makes connections between animation and other kinds of art in which artists invest materials with unexpected qualities. In her essay, she explores some of the curatorial questions that animation provokes for the gallery context and how ideas of animation can be extended beyond the moving image.

Ian White takes concepts of animation to its dark conclusion through its implied suggestions of control and order. Looking at three artists not known as 'animators', he proposes an opening up of the definition of animation to incorporate visual arts that would not ordinarily be considered as such.

The book begins with Edwin Carels tracing the historical oscillation between art and animation and meditating on where and how they meet and diverge – a key ongoing concern of the whole animate! project.

animate! was conceived by David Curtis, then Artists' Film and Video Officer at the Arts Council, and Clare Kitson, the Commissioning Editor for Animation at Channel 4, following conversations with producer Keith Griffiths. At different times, Dick Arnall, Maggie Ellis, Jacqui Davies and Jem Legh have contributed greatly to the success of the project. Since 2000, animate! has been produced through Finetake Limited, and its development and direction led by Dick Arnall's tireless commitment and rogue vision.

Benjamin Cook, Director of LUX, co-editor
Ruth Fielding, Lupus Films, Animation Consultant to Channel 4
Gary Thomas, Head of Moving Image, Arts Council England, co-editor

Endnotes

1 animate! commissioning guidelines

10/Cowboys Phil Mulloy (1991)

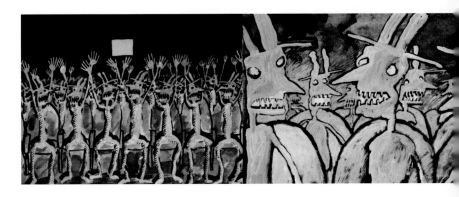

Animation = A Multiplication of Artforms?
Edwin Carels

Animation and art are often discussed as 'art and animation', as both together and apart. But when was the last time that anyone spoke of 'art and sculpture' or 'art and painting'? The term 'art and animation' suggests a kind of uncertainty, a hesitation about the status of animation as a real artform. Can we even talk about animation in such general terms? Surely it is too rich and complex a territory to be treated as a separate genre and is not a genre, but an artform in its own right. Just as cinema is not an art by definition, nor is animation. The underlying question of 'art and animation' is: How do you define which animated film is art and which is not? That is a very complicated affair and is a matter of context, of certain (and uncertain) criteria and mostly of authoritative voices.

In Russia, animation is called 'multiplikatsija' - a much more cooler sounding technical term than the more spiritually resonant word 'animation'. The idea of 'multiplikatsija' is not so much that it takes a multiplication of influences from other artforms to beget a new artform, instead it quite simply suggests the physiological effect that each film produces, which animation makes us more aware of: the projection of a multiplication of impressions on our retina, and thus on our mind.

Animation is the art of the interval. It all depends upon the eyes and the open mind of the viewer, the participation of each individual in the audience. It is a matter of spectatorship. Norman McLaren is most often cited for his motto: 'Animation is not the art of drawings that move, but the art of movements that are drawn. What happens between each frame is much more important than what exists on each frame. Animation is therefore the art of manipulating the invisible interstices that lie between the frames.' That is what McLaren thought was 'the philosophy behind his machine, the rostrum camera'. Animation according to McLaren is the art of the invisible becoming visible in the mind, and that is something quite different to blatantly referencing existing artworks and other artforms, as McLaren occasionally did

himself (for example making quite explicit his admiration of the surrealist painter Yves Tanguy, in some of his films).

Mental Frameworks

McLaren wanted his dictum to be understood not only in a technical but also in a metaphorical way. An animated film activates a whole mental framework, maybe as many as 24 frames a second. Animation, better than live action, demonstrates how our mind works, how it processes images and ideas. However, what McLaren quite intuitively describes still needs a lot of elaboration. For although a great deal of critical writing about animation has been produced in recent years, it is still not dealt with anywhere near as seriously as cinema is. And for that to happen we would need texts that investigate all the factors that come into play when an animated film is being received by a person's mind. So...

Animation functions as multiplication of stimuli: visual, perceptive, cognitive, art historical, technological, emotional, physical, social, economical, racial, gender-based, psychological, biographical, religious and gastronomical… to name but a few. For several decades film theory has demonstrated how many factors come into play when we try to gather meaning from a film, but it's only recently that some of this thinking has come to be applied to animated films.

Jean-Luc Godard famously proclaimed that cinema is the truth, 24 times a second. Paraphrasing McLaren, one could say: animation is the dark interval, 25 times a second. I'm not quite sure if Godard would still say that his video work *Histoire(s) du Cinéma* represents the truth, 24 times a second (although it indeed features a considerable amount of philosophical truths); if anything, with *Histoire(s) du Cinéma* Godard tried to re-animate his personal recollection of film history, in both a literal and in a figurative sense. The work is all post-production, playing with rhythms, with flicker. In short, every image is manipulated and made into a personal truth. One could say *Histoire(s) du Cinéma* is Godard's great work of animation, but obviously no theorist as yet has given that much thought.

So how is it that only the occasional animation artist is referenced in discussions about the art of cinema? It is well-known that for Godard and his fellow writers, critics and

Histoire(s) du Cinéma, Jean-Luc Godard (1988-1998)/15

filmmakers involved in the influential cinema magazine *Cahiers du Cinéma*, their experiences at the Paris Cinemathèque just after the Second World War were crucial. It is also known that they sometimes went to the Brussels Cinemathèque to see particular films, a venue where animation was regularly exhibited and Disney's *Fantasia* (1940) was shown alongside experimental animation works by artists such as Oskar Fischinger and the Russian Mikhail Tsekhanovsky.

There was a particular appreciation of animated art in Europe between the wars. Especially in Weimar Germany with the historic screening on 3rd May 1925 in Berlin, where the German avant-garde films of Hans Richter, Walter Ruttmann and Viking Eggeling were combined with the French Dadaist, or Surrealist or Cubist films of René Clair, Fernand Leger and Dudley Murphy. Most of them were artists who took up the camera rather than trained filmmakers. All sorts of avant-gardisms flourished, the first film clubs were started and the first theories on the cinema were produced. Never was the excitement over the seventh art so great as it was in that period. But by the early 30s, pivotal figures such as Oskar Fischinger were fleeing from Europe to the United States.

Ontological Truth

But let's get back to the rediscovery and re-valorisation of film by the critics – film as art in the post war sense. The writers of *Cahiers du Cinéma* approached cinema as a popular art and thus primarily focused on narrative film. A possible explanation for the initial lack of interest in animation might have been the influence of André Bazin, and his stress on the ontological truth of the photographic image. In animation, the status of the image is of course entirely different, particularly within cartoons, where every aspect of the image is constructed with no direct indexical relationship to the reality of the outside world. What stopped animation being accepted as a legitimate artform in the wider context was perhaps that it could not be incorporated within the fierce critical debate about the status and the (moral) implications of the image, as was the case with the photographic image of '*le cinema d'auteur*' when it started to become cultivated by French film magazines.

François Truffaut (1) made it clear that Hitchcock was more than an entertainer, and in fact a great artist, but did the same thing happen with any animator? The fact is that immediately after the war if there was any serious and enthusiastic attention given to animation, it usually went to Walt Disney. One of the very first European books on animation, on its history, its techniques and aesthetics, is by Lo Duca (2), co-founder of *Cahiers du Cinéma* with André Bazin and Jacques Doniol-Valcroze. Published in 1948, it includes an introduction by Walt Disney himself, in which he takes great pride in his own achievements and in the universal appeal and the universal potential of 'his' medium. Lo Duca himself sketches a broader picture of the history of animation and also of the situation at the time, but clearly his strongest admiration is for the work of Disney. He is not uncritical, as he rejects *Fantasia* not only for its pedantic tone, but also for its badly masked recuperation of abstract cinema and a stylisation that verges on picture postcard kitsch. Early in the book Lo Duca admits that some consider Disney the 'Raphaël of bad taste' but on the same page he stresses that in the future, honourable comparisons will be made between Goya and Disney, when looking at *Skeleton Dance*. But when it comes to *Fantasia*, he admits that the more consciously Disney wants to make art, the further removed he gets from it.

Nevertheless, Disney achieved something enormous according to Lo Duca. He used animation for what it can do best. In *Fantasia*, Lo Duca underlines that the film has succeeded in creating an admirable synthesis between many forms and techniques, from neons and microscopic imagery to William Blake's engravings, to the films of Painlevé and the 'pin-board' of Alexeieff – namely a multiplication of optical approaches. The year Lo Duca's praise of Disney was published, was also the year Sergei Eisenstein died. From 1940 until 1948, the Russian director worked on notes to compile a book on Disney, but as with so many of his writings, it was left unfinished. We do have the very strong opening line however, where Eisenstein states that: 'The work of this master is the greatest contribution of the American people to art.' So Eisenstein was clearly convinced that Disney was/is art. And just like Lo Duca, he admires Disney most for all the associations these films provoke in his well-educated mind. Eisenstein is – in his own words – mostly interested in the 'musical similarities of polysemantically flowing meanings in the elusive definition of words.' *Fantasia* he considers 'an experiment in the realisation of synthesis through syncretism.' But only a great, cultivated mind like Eisenstein's could elaborate so widely on the potential of this new art, and fill the intervals with such a wild and exciting stream of consciousness. But let it be clear, even if Eisenstein wrote one of the most enthusiast letters of noblesse for this new artform, in his texts we are admiring Eisenstein more than Disney.

In 1961, Robert Benayoun, like Lo Duca, a film lover with a strong interest in and devotion to surrealist art, published a book on animation after Disney (3). Benayoun is also somebody who, in his writing, clearly enjoys getting carried away by words and comparisons. One of his more famous statements is: 'Only animation has mobilised absurdity with perfect coherence.' And although he published a monograph on Tex Avery in 1988, he had already worked to give this name the status of an auteur in France as far back as the 1950s. Existentialism was the philosophy of the time, and the absurd, paranoid worldview of Avery's work apparently catered to that. In 1951 Benayoun started writing Avery letters and in 1962 he eventually tracked him down, when Avery's career was already well in decline. Luckily *Positif*, a rival film magazine to *Cahiers du Cinéma*, did focus regularly on animation and Benayoun could publish his writing there. As Benayoun did with Jerry Lewis, he lifted Tex Avery up into the pantheon of the auteurs and got his work accepted as art, just as Truffaut did with Hitchcock.

Self Promotion

The main reason why most people, in spite of so many wonderful and more adult alternatives, like the work of the Fleischers (creators of Betty Boop), kept on associating the art of animation with Disney was because the company had established such a powerful brand. From his *Silly Symphonies* (1934) series onwards, Disney perfectly understood how to do his own PR and how to proclaim himself as the inventor of a new art. Indeed, he did add a lot to the technological vocabulary and was equally a perfectionist on a stylistic level. How many animation artists were publishing books about themselves, or had them published? For example, since 1975, every couple of years new updates appear of *The Art of Walt Disney* by Christopher Finch, with Mickey Mouse artfully posing with a brush in his hands on the cover. In 1998 the same author also wrote a guide to animation art for Sotheby's auction house.(4) In it, he does not talk exclusively about Disney, but nevertheless, the predominance is very clear. The book starts with the question: 'What is animation art?' And then he gives the answer: 'Animation art is a term used to describe any of the many forms of artwork that are involved in the

making of an animated film. The example best known to the general public is the cel.' So, in collector's terms, the art of animation is everything except the movement. You can sell cells, but you cannot sell intervals. Obviously in English 'art' can mean artefact, as well as it can refer to a particular technique or express a particular quality.

In the fifth (not the very latest) edition of David Bordwell and Kristin Thompson's key film studies textbook *Film Art, an Introduction*, Walt Disney is mentioned only once in the index. Nevertheless, it is clear that Bordwell and Thompson's interest in animation is getting stronger with each edition. In 1979, when the first version of *Film Art* appeared, they mentioned animation in a scant three pages. By the second edition this had increased to five. In the third edition 14 pages dealt, at least in part, with the subject. By 1993, the fourth edition contained 36 pages with references to animation, and included a section devoted to separate analyses of three animated films: Disney's *Clock Cleaners* (1937), Chuck Jones's *Duck Amuck* (1953) and Robert Breer's *Fuji* (1974). However, in the fifth edition of *Film Art*, these analyses disappeared again, but there were more colour stills of avant-garde films. If we also take a look at the consecutive editions of their book *Film History - an Introduction* we notice that Bordwell and Thompson increasingly recognise the importance, popularity and the influence of animated cinema, avant-garde and experimental cinema. This has to do with the fact that since the 'digital revolution' animated special effects have become so dominant in live action cinema; to the point that on the cover of one of the most recent editions of *Film Art* we find a famous still from *The Matrix* (1999), with the special 'bullet time' effect.

So the standard textbooks on film are giving more and more attention to animation. But will the work by the Polish animator Jerzy Kucia ever find a place in this; and why doesn't Igor Kovalyov get the same recognition as, say, David Lynch? The answer of course is very simple: film critics and historians hardly get to see this kind of animation and so they cannot cultivate its reputation as art. It all starts with festivals, where one supposedly goes to make discoveries. As a journalist interested in both fields, for years it was an imposs-ible choice between the animation festival in Annecy and the Cannes film festival, as they both took place at the same time. Even an animator like Jan Svankmajer clearly preferred to go to Cannes, once invited there with his work. A film needs media attention to gain instant recognition, and prizes at festivals also play an important part in this. Ultimately an audience will look to a voice of authority to institutionalise something into art.

Poètes Maudits

A specialist animation festival such as Annecy is perhaps not the ideal territory to get recognition as an important artist. In 1993 the work of animator William Kentridge was introduced at Annecy, however it wasn't until four years later that he became internationally renowned by way of the international art circuit. He was shown at Documenta X in Kassel where his work demonstrated one of the ambitions of Documenta in a clear way: how to respond to the visual overload of the media and create strong potent images as a counterweight in the information society. But another criteria cannot be underestimated: the biography of the artist. Kentridge is the son of an important lawyer and as such a privileged witness to crucial changes in his country, South Africa. That clearly marks his works, no matter how subjective and associative they may seem. Jerzy Kucia doesn't have such a dramatic biography. If the genius is not a poète maudit, his chances of get attention automatically become smaller.

The Estonian Priit Pärn gained notoriety, not only because of the quality of his master-piece *Breakfast on the Grass* (1987), but also because of the timeliness of this work in the context of Perestroika. Luckily, Pärn's films are available on DVD – and another simple factor for a significant artist to gain recognition is that it's easier if your admirers can buy something and show it to other people. Kentridge is a clear example of an artist who produces 'pieces' and installations that can be promoted in galleries, again a problem for Kucia who doesn't have such representation. Every visual artist knows that to get into a museum, one has to pass through the gallery system first. There are some exceptions and also a historical precedent: in the 1940s, Solomon Guggenheim gave grants to animators Norman McLaren, Oskar Fischinger, and John and James Whitney. Since the centenary of the cinema, museums are more than ever prepared to turn their white spaces into black boxes to welcome all sorts of projections

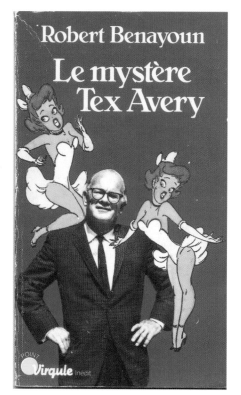

and installations with moving images. Cinema is being reinvented by young artists who don't really know much about the past, and the same goes for animation: it is considered hip, as long as it is young and fresh.

Would the Quay Brothers ever be nominated for the Turner Prize and why didn't the critics welcome Martin Creed's prize-winning work *#227* as a form of expanded animation? In the past, some artists found their way out of the animation ghetto and into the art world quite spontaneously. The exhibition *Force Fields: Phases of the Kinetic* at the Hayward Gallery, London in 2000 used a kinetic sculpture by Len Lye as the key image in all the publicity. In the exhibition there were also projections of James Whitney's animated films *Lapis* (1963-66) and *Yantra* (1950-57). An earlier important show on kinetic art in London, in 1970, featured Robert Breer, another example of someone who was already considered part of more than one movement as well as a significant avant-garde filmmaker, and who had mostly used the single frame animation technique, since the 1950s. Len Lye preferred to call himself a 'motion composer' rather than an artist or filmmaker. And maybe that term works just as well for the Quay Brothers, as they also work in the theatre, opera and dance as composers of calligraphic spaces.

Bachelor Machines

Many artists are hard to situate in the interval between live action and animation, between animation and the visual arts, between animation and illustration, even though the art world has been more open towards multi-media work. Maybe it's better not to speak about animation as such anymore. Look at how video art has largely disappeared as a term, but as a medium is now being used more than ever.

For instance, why can't we consider an animated film a 'bachelor machine' as we can a large piece of glass, the most classic example being Marcel Duchamp's *The Large Glass*? The films of the Quay Brothers particularly deserve to be reconsidered under this respect. Duchamp is well-known for his rejection of retinal art, but at the same time was fascinated by optical phenomena. Anamorphosis, stereoscopy, rotoreliefs, the effect of complementary colours… a lot of his work is inspired optical phenomena that also forms the basis of (pre-)cinematic inventions. (In recent years Kentridge's interest in this has become clearer as well.) Duchamp's idea of a post-retinal art leaves a lot to the viewer, it is up to the viewer to make the connections on *The Large Glass*, to mentally animate the suggested movement. Duchamp also cultivated the notion of the in-between and/or the 'infrathin', that which allows the mind of the beholder to come up with a fertile stream of associations.

One could abandon the term animation and look for another, more encompassing one, or one could be as purist as possible and try to single out, so to speak, the unique selling proposition of the particular artform. As we have seen, 'art' can be understood as many things – on a material, technical or aesthetic level. Although one can disagree on the purely artistic results of his many experiments, fundamentally McLaren's 'philosophy behind the machine' still holds: that animation is above all the art of the in-between, of the interval, of the beholder, of the mental movement, the stream of consciousness, the free flow of associations. It is the art of reading between the lines. It is not about the art that is on the image, but about the art that emerges between the images. A multiplication of impressions on the mind.

Emile Cohl and Marcel Duchamp were not of the same age, but they were contemporaries nonetheless, peaking in their careers at around the same period and both were very critical about the state of the art that surrounded them. Emile Cohl was a key figure of the Incoherents movement before the Dadaists were even born and his very first film, *Fantasmagorie* (1908) is still striking today for its sheer liberty of imagination. Cohl, like Winsor McCay, like Disney, and like many other pioneers of the art of animation, had an earlier career as a cartoonist, making caricatures. Their first films appeared like delirious lightning sketches, demonstrations of how fast the mind could hop from one idea to another. One could claim that the Quay Brother's *In Absentia* (2000) is also such a lightning sketch and it is also very explicitly a film about writing with light. It is, in a sense, putting the 'graph' back in to the 'cinématographe'. Great artists often reinvent the medium they work in. Cinema was invented as a graphic technique, to register movement and then to reproduce it. Now, in the era of computer graphics, the time is ripe to accept that all moving images are only on some level indexical and that they are, foremost, illusions. Films are mental constructions and therefore very personal and complex constellations, both in the literal and in the figurative sense a projection.

Endnotes

1 See Truffaut, François, *The Cinema According to Alfred Hitchcock*, 1967, revised edition known as *Truffaut-Hitchcock*, Simon & Schuster, 1985
2 Lo Duca, *Le Dessin Animé. Histoire Esthetique Technique*, Prisma, 1948
3 Benayoun, Robert, *Le Dessin Animé Après Walt Disney*, Pauvert, 1961
4 Finch, Christopher and Rosenkrantz, Linda, *Sotheby's Guide to Animation Art*, Henry Holt & Company, 1988

save me

① I AM IN TROUBLE

OH NO
I'm A SUPERMODE

This is your
Lucky Day
Simon

SIMON

BANNERS
BEHIND ME
MAKE ME
STRONG

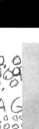

Artist Interviews *Mike Sperlinger*

AL + AL

AL + AL met in a chance encounter whilst visiting Derek Jarman's Garden in Dungeness in 1997. Having subsequently graduated together in Fine Art from Central St Martins School of Art in 2001, they received studio awards from ACAVA and Acme to build a live-and-work blue screen video studio in London. From this blue screen void, AL + AL have programmed and produced a body of video work which uses computer generated environments to provide simulated contexts for their studio performances. They have exhibited internationally in galleries, film festivals, cinemas and on television and will have their first international touring solo show opening at FACT in Liverpool in 2007.

AL + AL's first film for animate!, Perpetual Motion in the Land of Milk and Honey (2004), was a re-fabrication of their grandfather's attempts to invent a perpetual motion machine. They are currently working on a new animate! project called Interstellar Stella.

MS: *How do you feel about being described as animators?*

A+A: The first time we thought about it was when we went to the animate! previews at Bradford Animation Festival and did a talk after the screening. Before that we'd never thought about it, but we started being asked these questions – we were quite freaked out! It was really strange to get all these young animators asking us about animation – 'What tools do you use?' and so on. We realised that the commission had taken us into a world which we hadn't realised we were part of – we didn't realise we were animators – because we'd come out of doing fine art at St Martins.

We'd started out by doing performance works with video cameras, which were very stripped-down performance works, very domestic, and we were considering all that 1960's video work like Bruce Nauman or Vito Acconci, thinking about documenting the artist's body in the studio space. That was how our practice began. Then we started thinking, 'Wouldn't it be interesting if we substituted something for the grotty studio…' which is kind of the gesture behind all that early 1960's work: that there's always this non-analysed space behind the performance, as if the artist's studio somehow isn't a space. So we wanted to consider that as a context in itself, to see if we could make our performances in a contextless space.

This work actually began for us with the blue screen. The very first time that we truly worked together, we made a 30-minute short film, with some blue screen work in it, and we had actors – it was completely different to anything we'd done before. The blue screen came out of that and so did the idea of exploring fictional spaces. But along the way we became obsessed with blue screen, not because we liked blue screen movies, but because we'd been to see *The Phantom Menace* (1999) and found it strange that the piece *was* a phantom: it seemed that all the performances weren't there. We were fascinated by that emptiness because that movie is really about fullness: the ecstasy of spectacle. It was very modern and very empty – we thought this was the most modern thing we'd ever seen. So we went away and thought, 'What would it be like to do some blue screen work?' The first thing we did was a performance where one of us played a blue screen set cleaner, and basically it's about Hoovering infinity. But it's also about the artist in the studio with nothing, with emptiness, with not knowing what to do, which goes right back to those Nauman performances – just the artist's body in the studio, marking out space. We thought we were just going to do one performance piece with blue screen and just leave it blue, and actually talk about that void space in itself being interesting rather than making it disappear for a spectacle.

MS: *At this point your interest wasn't at all in the digital possibilities, it was in that complete blankness?*

A+A: Yes, totally. And we thought about the technology too. When artists in the 60s, 70s and 80s were making those video works, that was the technology that was around – to actually have a video camera was quite a big deal, even in the 80s. When we were working in video, around 1999, you could actually get your hands on a proper editing system for a computer. So technology had moved on from when people like Nauman were making work, and we felt that we weren't pushing it, we weren't being honest about the technology. We felt like we weren't being contemporary artists. We realised we were just filming the body in space, but that we weren't taking it anywhere. Technology started to turn its volume up in our minds and that's where our obsession with the essence of technology came in – through the blue screen, through that technological void – technology become a huge question for us.

Another aspect was that we could take performances and change the way we saw them, by changing the context, as we could actually simulate any context – we could

Hoover in a jail, or we could Hoover in a *Star Wars* set. The performance changes its meaning, its resonances, through these different contexts. Blue screen enabled us to document performing with our bodies in the studio, but then to work beyond that to find ways in which to contextualise the performance, in ways that we might not have considered when we were performing.

Now you know why we didn't see ourselves as animators. Because when we were at art school, we weren't thinking about bringing an inanimate object to life – we were thinking of performance and the history of video art, and not Walt Disney… It was after the Bradford Animation Festival that we came back and really wanted to look up all these animators. We felt like we'd found another audience, and they were fascinated by us because we were talking in this different language, but at the same time it applied to them – they were very interested in what we were saying.

MS: *Insofar as you think animation is something distinct from art, what do you think it is?*

A+A: We had this conversation with the curator Edwin Carels and he was trying to propose that Martin Creed's light going on and off is a piece of animation, which we think is absolutely true in the sense that there is a philosophical, critical language which can be applied to the word 'animation'. The liberation of the word animation is actually an interesting project. But when you first say the word, it makes you think of the 50 people that programme *Star Wars*, or who make a video game, or who make an advert…

MS: *It's kind of industrial…*

A+A: That's it, because it's so industrialised – because it can be industrialised in a way that perhaps all forms can be. But it's slippery ground… We just know that we're not animators. But it's to do with the conversation in the studio, where the index isn't animation – it's a contemporary art show we've just been to, or all the big daddies that we love like Warhol or Duchamp. They're the people who are in the studio and we don't really think of them as animators. So the animate! scheme brought that word to the studio.

MS: *So how did* Perpetual Motion, *your first animate! film, start out?*

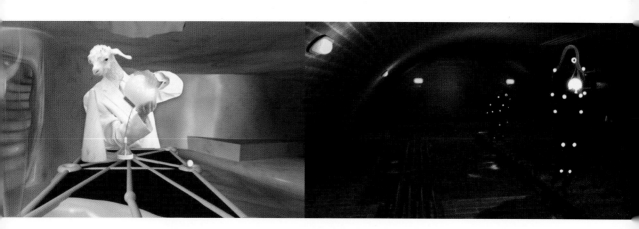

A+A: When we first set out we were making a project about my granddad, whose project was almost communist in the sense that his ideology was that he wanted to make a perpetual motion device, the holy grail of engineering, so that everyone could have free power. No one would need oil, no one would need corporations – the project is beautiful in that it is a metaphor of power, on all sorts of levels…

MS: *And he began this project around the time of the Jarrow marches?*

A+A: Exactly, in the 1930s. And we felt close to it because we felt like industrial revolution slaves – we grew up in terraced houses, inside Accrington brick, and at one time we would have been working from eight-years-old making cotton for Victorian millionaires – all these ideologies came out of that landscape.

So we'd been commissioned to make a piece about my granddad inventing perpetual motion. And the animate! thing is great, because you are making a work for television. We didn't really think about that before we got involved, but when we suddenly realised, 'We're making a piece for television', we found that absolutely fascinating. Up until that point we'd only ever done site-specific installations and gallery shows, and we'd come out of this fine art language. We knew that fine artists had made pieces for television before and we'd seen things like Richard Billingham's *Fish Tank* (2000), and David Hall's work – lots of people had made things for television. But animate! was giving us access to this incredible space. Television is so much a part of all our lives.

MS: *And what effect did that have on the work – did you start to think of it as being an intervention into television?*

A+A: We first realised that we hadn't considered the context of television about halfway through making *Perpetual Motion*. Then we knew it wasn't rigorous enough, that it was too easy, and our heads fell off. One of the main things we thought about was the speed. We thought that people would turn off at what we were making, they'd flip channels. A gallery is kind of like a cottonwool world – someone going into a gallery thinks they're going to give something time, whereas when you switch the television on, you just don't think that. Clearly artists in the past had thought that they could make, let's call them difficult works, and you'd used the word 'intervention' – so when you put a tap dripping on the television you're saying something about the space of television and

what other programmes are like, or what time is like on television. But we weren't happy with that – in a way we wanted television to intervene in our work, rather than the other way around. We felt that if we did something like that, people wouldn't watch it, so what's the point in making it? We'd have already lost, we'd be making it for nobody – which artists don't do, really.

This made us think, 'We're not doing very well here, as artists. We've got this commission and we're just plodding away, making a piece just like normal.' When we're making a piece for an installation or gallery, we're completely rigorous – we're thinking about the whole space, the context, who we're showing with, what the show is going to be called, all of those things. And yet, when we were making a piece for television it was as if we didn't need to think about that – and then suddenly we realised we did.

That's when the Britney Spears thing came in. At that time she was on the television a lot, with her extraordinary video [*Toxic*]. We thought, 'This is television', and philosophically it worked in our minds – what she represented as a symbol, and what granddad's project of perpetual motion was... We realised that all these celebrities that invade this space are searching for infinity, for a fame that will last beyond their death – for a kind of perpetual motion. But at the same time, they're a kind of cog in this perpetual motion device of capitalism.

We decided to sabotage our own work or to allow something that was already on television to sabotage our minds.

MS: *Is that what you mean about television intervening into your work?*

A+A: Yes, in a way Britney Spears became this floating spirit of capitalism all the way through this world that we were exploring that granddad's communist project got lost in. But also, at the moment that we thought the viewer was going to turn over to watch MTV instead of us, we turned over for them – we saw it as being like channel hopping. The ocean sequence before Britney Spears appears is actually the pace the whole piece was going to be originally – very slow, very fluid – and then she comes in and it turns into the pop video. It's actually a frame-by-frame appropriation of her video, we analysed all her moves, and so in a way it's a kinetic analysis of the infinite glitter of merchandise. By a complete coincidence, granddad had 'toxic' written on his shed door – so when we saw that, we knew it was right!

MS: *Watching it again, I noticed the theme of puppetry and control with the Lamb*

Perpetual Motion in the Land of Milk and Honey (2004) AL + AL/33

character – is that partly a kind of self-reflexivity about your position as authors? Because you are creating everything out of nothing using the blue screen and taking on this slightly god-like role…

A+A: We perform all of the parts, so there is that connection to us, but the Lamb is like a controller – all our works have a controller in them. That does come up in animators' language a lot too, being able to control everything and make everything happen, and that's slipped into our language. Every frame you see of ours we've made a decision about.

MS: *The idea of creating out of nothing, out of the void, is very important to you.*

A+A: We were thinking again about someone like Nauman and those fantastic performances and we thought, 'Did he really want that rubbish in the back corner? What does that rubbish mean – is it just to be ignored, is it there or not?' These questions about the context of everything that was in the frame began to really motivate us, to the extent that we began to question it about all artists that use film – we started to ask, why have they considered one part of the frame and not another? They weren't in control of the street scene behind where they're filming and so on. So part of how we became seduced by the idea of making everything, was so that when you looked at every frame of our work you knew that the artist had decided the colour, the material – it's like painting in that respect. We know you can say that about all video artists or all filmmakers, but we always get this feeling that even when you're watching a film where it's a complete set, you're never quite sure who made the set. It would be like going to a Joseph Beuys installation and not being quite sure if he'd rolled the felt – it sounds ridiculous, but we feel it's important. Of course, there are artists like Matthew Barney who use massive crews, or Jeff Koons – it's not that we're anti that.

There's also the question about authorship, because there's been a big conversation since the 1970s about the death of the author, not just in terms of writing but in terms of the artist too. And in many ways that question is also linked to technology, because of the idea of tools that almost make things themselves. There is this sense when some people watch our films they think machines do everything, they genuinely do – but it interests us that someone might think that, because they're actually looking at something so authored that it's almost from another time, a time earlier than that

conversation. So we like that conflicting message in the work, that at one level it looks like we're making something that's so radically hands-off and yet at the same time we've actually sculpted and painted everything you see.

MS: *But you still both appear in the works as performers, rather than using complete simulacra – you maintain the sense of bodies in space.*

A+A: Yes, that's right. We have used animated characters once or twice, but that's the point where we start to feel like animators, funnily enough. That's not to say that if an object appears in a scene it's not animated – a tree, for example, might move in the wind – but there's something about making a person lift their hand up or something which feels strange.

We actually did it to our own bodies in *Perpetual Motion*. When we analysed Britney Spears' performance frame-by-frame, we had to appropriate that – we had to call her gait inside ourselves, if you like, and embody that kind of kinetic seduction. That in itself was a kind of artist's project – a kind of ridiculous analysis through imitation of the performance – it was a study of the way in which this seduction is constructed. But ironically what came out of that was this piece that was perfect for television.

I think that's why we were so interested in the animate! scheme and why we applied again, because we felt that we'd made a work that was formally our most resolved and yet also our most seductive – our most modern piece.

MS: *So with your new commission, how do you feel your approach has changed?*

A+A: For the new one, we're making a piece called *Interstellar Stella*. Again it's about a family member, this time it's about our niece Megan who's a child model. Effectively, we're making the piece about photographs – it's another thing about technology in a way, why we give ourselves over to making images and why there are some people who don't think images are good. When we went home, we were faced with these images of Megan at home and on billboards and everything. So we realised that Megan is an ideal subject for this idea of 'mediated being'. We've given our lives over to living inside this blue void, living on both sides of the glass, inside a simulation – and we realised that Megan's doing the same. But we had issues – we thought, 'Is it good that she's doing this as a child and going to different male photographers and being used as an object

to sell objects?' That's how it started, her career was challenging to us and that this was real territory for us to make a new piece with animate! Now that we're inside it, we've realised that there's a bigger piece of work about those first thoughts – why did we think that? Why would it be bad for a little girl to have her photograph taken?

It made sense for us to go back to animate! for the commission. All Megan knows is advertising, and of course Channel 4 is a commercial station with adverts in between the programmes. That's part of the context of Megan's childhood, so we wanted to make a piece of work where we showed her how we make work and how it's completely different to that, and how she could become an author – we bought her a camera for Christmas. Seeing her with a camera, we realised that she'd gained the skill through having her photograph taken, not only of being an object, but of taking pictures herself. So when she takes the standard family picture, aged eight and a half, she's completely orchestrating it, as if she's a professional. That whole *X-Factor* aspect to childhood we do find fascinating. Television offers the ideal context for this piece, which the gallery couldn't really offer us.

MS: *Who else is making work at the moment that's an influence for you?*

A+A: One of our most important artists is Mike Nelson. He made us discover context-lessness – he changed space itself, the gallery space, to the extent that it was like reading a novel. With a show like *The Coral Reef* at Matt's Gallery, he made us start to see that we could make space become as important as the performance. But the conversation in the studio isn't just about contemporary art, because a lot of contemporary art disappoints us, so there's also a sense of communing with the dead in our work – the blue screen is a kind of death as well. For example, Beuys believed that his felt saved his life and we feel that our blue felt is the kind of dark sister of that. In some ways, we've substituted life for a simulation.

We feel that all blue screen performances are in this space without time or place. If you look at the blue screen footage from Cecil B. DeMille's *Ten Commandments* (1956), or the blue screen footage from *The Phantom Menace*, it looks like it's in the same place at the same time – but it's 50 years and thousand of miles apart. So dead artists are a part of that conversation: Yves Klein does speak out of the blue to us about blue screen, and Derek Jarman does with his *Blue* (1993), and Michelangelo with his *Last Judgement* blue – we see that as a proto-blue screen work.

Paul Bush

Paul Bush was born in 1956 and studied Fine Art at Central School of Art and Design and at Goldsmiths College, London. He taught himself how to make films while a member of the London Film-makers' Co-op and Chapter Film Workshop in Cardiff. As well as producing his own animations through his production company Ancient Mariner Productions, he makes commercials for Picasso Pictures and has taught and given workshops at art colleges internationally. In 1999, he polled second in Creation magazine's annual list of animation directors.

His first film for animate! was His Comedy (1994), an adaptation of Gustave Doré's illustrations for Dante's The Divine Comedy made by scratching directly into the surface of 35mm colour filmstock to recreate the style of the original engravings. His second animate! production was Furniture Poetry (1999), a frame-by-frame animation in which objects and furniture are constantly changing their shapes. Both films have won prizes at festivals around the world.

MS: *You've made a huge variety of work, so to what extent do you think of yourself as an animator?*

PB: It's very difficult, because I don't really think of myself as an animator, but the fact is I'm always teaching animation and lecturing to animators much more than to filmmakers.

MS: *So other people tend to classify you as an animator?*

PB: Exactly – and it feels rather rude to say you're not, when you're talking to people who actually really want to be animators!

It's partly because I'm not just doing animation and I don't want to just do animation. It's also because, except for one or two notable exceptions, I don't do drawn animation. Even *His Comedy* and *The Albatross* (1998), which appear graphic, in actual fact, are made by tracing over live action images. There are only two films that haven't involved live action: *Geisha Grooming* (2003) which I did with Lisa Milroy, where she did the drawings and I just animated it, and *Flik-Flak* (2000) with Phil Mulloy, where we designed it together. Those are the only two which are graphic; all the work I've done on my own has some kind of photographic image – it may be single frame and it may have stuff on top of it – but it's basically photographic. Because the one thing I find totally and utterly important to me about film is photography.

I was discussing this the other day at the Norwich Animation Festival, because I feel that animators tend to come to animation through fine art, and their idea of animation is to try to get movement into drawing of some sort – to extend drawing into time. My relationship to animation is actually to take film – moving photographic images – and to take that apart, to reduce it in some way down to the smallest particle. I'm reducing *down* from film, whereas I think most animators are building *up* from the still image.

MS: *Do you feel connected more to someone like, say, Eadweard Muybridge, than the names most people in animation would invoke?*

PB: Well, I think Muybridge didn't know what he was doing! He didn't know what consequences it would have for film and animation. I'm sure he had no idea that his books would become textbooks that animators would look at in order to study movement. But my whole background in film, learning film, was though looking at work of the 1970s, primarily by American experimental movie-makers – some of whom, like Paul Sharits and Stan Brakhage, were doing single frame work. Also Tony Conrad, and later Chris Welsby – there's no way that Chris Welsby would call himself an animator, but he did do a lot of single frame work and time lapse.

MS: *So your influences came from quite a specific area of filmmaking, rather than from the general history of animation – in particular via the London Film-makers' Co-op.*

PB: Yes, that was where I learnt to make films and that's when I was suddenly discovering lots of people who had made films which played around with time, and the single frame is a fantastic tool for exploring time.

MS: *Would anyone have talked about these films in terms of animation?*

PB: No, not really. I think there were one or two people specifically doing animation at

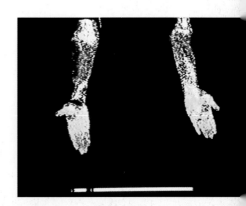

the Co-op and I didn't identify with them at all – I wasn't doing that kind of work.

The other interesting thing is that I very rarely show my animation work and my non-animation work together, partly out of my own choice; I do sometimes show *Rumour of True Things* (1996), which isn't animation but does have lots of single frame stuff in it, as part of a programme of my animation work. But a year or so ago I did show a mixed programme at Kingston College, and someone from the audience pointed out that all my early work tended to be of very long duration shots – I was very influenced by Jean-Marie Straub, for example. Straub had these shots that were held for an enormous length of time, so long that sometimes you actually started noticing the grain of the film – they were held too long for the information that they imparted. And then, without doing any films with normal kind of cutting in between, I ended up making films in which every frame changed.

It's at the edges that film tends to reveal itself as an artificial construction – it tends to be when you hold shots too long or if you start breaking it down to the single frame. They're at completely different ends of the spectrum, but they're actually achieving a similar thing, which is to reveal the artificiality of film.

MS: *How much was your background in fine art an influence on your filmmaking?*

PB: I think it informed, or cemented, an aesthetic about how things should be visually, particularly about economy. At Goldsmiths we had a lot of teachers who were involved in Conceptualism and Minimalism, that was the ethos. The king then was Jasper Johns. It wasn't necessarily that I was going to carry on doing the kind of work I did in college, but I learnt things like economy of means, absolutely the opposite to Baroque and Rococo. Because there's another strong movement in avant-garde filmmaking which is psychodrama – Kenneth Anger, Jack Smith, George Kuchar, Derek Jarman – that kind of aesthetic was the complete opposite to what I was doing.

MS: *If you were trying to characterise your work generally, including the animated and the non-animated, do you think it's possible to identify common concerns?*

PB: I think it's a mixture of things. Going back to this thing about Minimalism, I do think that the reworking of things that already exist is something that's always interested me. I remember a film I saw from the American experimental movement, *Tom Tom the Piper's*

Son (1969-71) by Ken Jacobs, where he reworked a tiny piece of found footage. He zoomed in, re-filmed little episodes and so on, and turned it into a two-hour film. So reworking something that already exists and not feeling that you have to produce something fresh, but rather to revisit something and re-present it, whether that's archive footage or a text or a Gustave Doré engraving – I think that's the common factor, something that's in all the films.

MS: *Looking back on the two films you made for* animate!, His Comedy *and* Furniture Poetry, *how do you feel about them now? Were they important films for you?*

PB: It's difficult to say whether one film or another is more important, but *His Comedy* was important because it was the first commission I'd made, and I had been making films for 14 years before getting that commission. It was incredible after such a long drought to be paid to make a film. And it did really change things for me because I gave up teaching, as a way of making a living, soon afterwards. That just changed my whole relationship to making films. It made it easier to make them and I was more pragmatic about it as well. Because the minute you start earning money from making films, it's quite important to finish them on time! When I was making films with my own money in the 1980s it was like, 'Well, I might as well keep on making it until it's perfect.' But when you're making it for someone else you have deadlines and while you're making it you know you only have income for a year or half a year.

It was amazing to make a film that people cared about or even knew that you were making! Because if you make a film with your own money, who knows, who cares, apart from you and your friends? It focuses your attention when you know there's a slot for it and it's going to be shown – that's quite a big difference.

Also, because it was animation, it was something that was accumulated over a long time in a different way to my previous films. It would accumulate just from me sitting at a desk. I had small children and I found it was a way of working that I really liked. It equated more to the art practices I'd been doing as a young adult, because I wasn't going off on location with the endless preparation for a week's shoot. It was a year where the film slowly accumulated and you were working all the time, and it was varied work. People probably don't think that when they look at it, but it was very varied – I was shooting a bit, I was scratching, working with the sound designer – there were lots of different things involved.

I also learnt that I was very good at working over a long period of time and, as I say to

people now doing animation, you've got to be someone who's into deferred gratification – there's no point doing animation if you're someone who wants to get results at the end of a day. Doing independent animation you've almost got to be two people: you've got to be the director, who has the idea and the vision for the project, and you've got to be the worker, the slave, the *animator.* You can't think about it critically, you've just got to work for as long as it takes to finish the project. Then you can be a director again and think about editing and sound, but you can't suddenly halfway through become the director again and think, 'Oh, this isn't a good project, I want to do another one.' You have to be in those two modes and I was very happy one moment to be someone with the ideas and then for a year just to sit down and slog away.

MS: Furniture Poetry *seems like it was a kind of a breakthrough film for you, in terms of your profile.*

PB: I think *His Comedy* was the breakthrough. Things did happen very quickly for me, but at quite a late age, whereas many animators who leave the Royal College of Art make one film and then they're working quite successfully. For me, it didn't happen until I was in my mid-thirties.

So *His Comedy* was the real breakthrough for me, and then soon after I did *Rumour of True Things* (1996), which was a kind of important in another way because it was hugely successful. Each time I did something different it felt like a huge risk, because after *His Comedy* it felt like I should spend the rest of my life scratching and establishing myself as an animator who used a particular technique, which is what lots of people do. So *Rumour of True Things* seemed a terrible risk, but I wanted very much to make it and I was given the money to make it. Then I did *The Albatross* and that was also significant as it's the film that all the animators like! The animation world likes *The Albatross* because it's a proper story and it's real hardcore animation, and it won a lot of prizes, so I became established in that world.

The thing about *Furniture Poetry* was that it looked again like I was just throwing that all away. I thought people would laugh it off, but it was also very successful in a different way, reaching a wider field than animation, through some of the experimental film festivals. Every time you make another film that people like to see, it seems to cement your position, which is always very vulnerable as an artist and self-employed person. But nothing really does cement your position, in the sense that I know people who've been incredibly successful for 10 or 15 years then have disappeared.

MS: *Are there people working at the moment whose work you're particularly excited by?*

PB: Yes, obviously there are – but I still feel a bit of an outsider. I'm more interested in cinema and live action films. There are a lot of people whose work I show to students, for example, who are making single frame work but don't think they're working in animation – people like Martin Arnold, for instance. It's on the fringes of the animation spectrum that I find work interesting, let's put it that way; it's where it touches on the photographic nature of film.

MS: *Is animation really just a label of convenience for you?*

PB: There's always been a big battle with these terms, less among the practitioners and more among the curators. As far as artists go, I don't think we like classifying our work! But there is a big battle for what animation should be – should it be cartoons, or cartoons and puppets, or should we let CGI in? And so on. What's happened is that the animation world has gradually accepted these new techniques, and for me to move into the animation world was to be allowed to make experiments and for people to want to see them. There are people who want the animation world to be very small and exclusively about cartoons, but they're in a minority, and that means that the animation arena has become very rich because lots of people with diverse practices have been included. That means the festivals are interesting, the college courses are interesting… And even understood conventionally, when you look at an animated feature compared to a live action feature the scope of the story is greater – because animation compresses time. An actor requires a certain amount of time to cross a room but a cartoon character can do it in a different way.

Certainly within British cinema, drama is rooted in neo-realism, and the notion of documentary is quite journalistic, not personal or essayistic, and there are limits in terms of the way that visual language is used to communicate. In animation that's blown open, because of this ability to squeeze and stretch action, movement and time, to use shorthand, to tell things with a single line – it's an arena where there seem to be fewer rules, and that's why I am working in animation. So I don't deny that I work in the animation field, it's just that the animation field has opened up for people to explore visual language in a way that's impossible in other areas.

Furniture Poetry Paul Bush (1999)

Ann Course

Ann Course was born in 1965 in Watford. She and her partner Paul Clark both studied at the Royal College of Art, and they now live and work in London. Ann's animations involve simple line drawings and photocopies edited together, employing the minimum of movement to suggest the maximum of disturbing ambiguities. As well as her videos, most of them made in collaboration with Paul, Ann makes sculptures and drawings. She has shown widely, including at Tate Britain, Whitechapel Art Gallery and had a 2005 solo show at Mercer Union in Toronto.

Rotting Artist (2002), their film for animate!, is a scatological symphony featuring coffins and a chimney brush, set to a Beethoven score.

MS: *What would be your first reaction to the word animation?*

AC: One of repulsion!

MS: *What do you associate with it?*

AC: I think it's to do with shame… I just think of it in straightforward repulsive terms – I don't want to think about it, basically, which is pretty bad isn't it? I think in general everyday life you probably get to see better quality feature films than you would animation, because animation's separated off into this kind of thing isn't it? Seeking out interesting animation is actually quite difficult.

MS: *Do you have a sense for yourself, then, of what animation is, how would you define it?*

AC: Well personally, although maybe it's a dull way to talk about it, I think any film could be an animation because it's just a selection of stills put together – and if I think about it like that, I can feel quite happy about it. I quite like flicker films, for example, where things just go on and off.

MS: *Are you an animator?*

AC: I wouldn't want to dictate how people describe me. People say all kinds of things to me, for example that my drawings are cartoons, which I don't necessarily like. But I think if that's what they think and that's the way they want to talk about it, I should be pragmatic rather than getting into a panic about it, thinking that it's going to dictate where I go if people refer to me in that way. But the reason that I've come to make animation is that I had all of these still drawings which, if they're put together one after the other, make different meanings or illuminate the meaning of the others.

MS: *Could you talk a little bit about your background as an artist, before you were making animation?*

AC: Well, I never thought I would go to art college and I actually asked my father for his permission to go – which I find really weird now. It was quite a last minute thing and first of all I got a certificate in vocational art and design. After that, I did a foundation course because I was interested in drawing and painting, which was really good. But then I spent three years out of college and I didn't get in to study fine art until an old tutor of mine encouraged me to apply for illustration. Illustration just seemed to fit my background: it was sensible and you could make some money. So I ended up doing a BA in Illustration at Chelsea, then I tried to transfer to do fine art because I didn't think I could deal with it, and then I had to have a year out. But it made sense to do illustration, because you could pretty much do what you wanted to on that course and nobody asked you any heavy questions about why you were doing it; so I actually had a lot of freedom. Whereas I think if I'd been on a fine art course and people had asked me why I was doing this and why I was doing that, I might have just cried.

In 1991, did a two-year MA in Illustration at the Royal College of Art. But I pretty much only worked in a sketchbook and it was after I left college that I started to draw from my imagination.

MS: *What kinds of things were you drawing before that?*

AC: I couldn't work from my imagination at all, because I found it a bit upsetting and incoherent and quite negative. I was trying to make things that looked acceptable to other people. I was hung up on this whole idea of skill – whereas now I know that the surface of the earth is just seething with super-talented, skilled people and you might

as well forget that. There's not much point in making something just to please somebody else and it's not necessarily going to get you anywhere.

MS: *Who were you interested in at the point, who influenced you?*

AC: Well I liked Van Gogh and Soutine – but my knowledge of art wasn't good until my foundation course. Then later, while Paul was at the Royal College and I was at Chelsea, he went to Paris and did a residency there and so I got to see a lot more contemporary work, people like Bruce Nauman.

MS: *So you were already working with Paul at this point?*

AC: We lived in a garret together! And we used to do things like go out oil painting together and bring home dead pigeons and do still life paintings on the weekend, stuff like that. I wanted to paint really, and I'd still like to get round to it, but I like to work for short periods of time – like 50 minutes, max.

MS: *It's funny that you've ended up in animation, because it has this reputation of taking months of work to produce a two-minute film…*

AC: Well I don't spend that much time – I make things very quickly. There's absolutely no reason why people should have to work like that and if it doesn't produce good results, why do people do it? It goes back to this idea of labouring over something to look like something else – wouldn't it be better just to think about it a bit more, before you even get out of bed?

MS: *So how did you start with animation?*

AC: At the Royal College of Art I made a sequence of 54 drawings, if I remember rightly. I'd traced them off and they were in the first film that I made, called *Ann(i)Mated* (1993). It's a picture of me at an exercise class, opening my legs. I put that down on a timeline at college and I thought, 'This is ridiculous – 54 drawings, I'm not doing that'. But then Andrzej Klimowski, who was a tutor, saw it and said he really liked it, so I thought, 'OK, there's got to be a quicker way of doing it.' So I just photocopied a drawing and

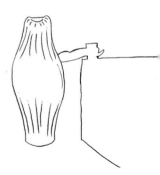

Tippex'd it out, moving the bits I wanted to move.

I would only ever move a drawing that had an obvious before or after moment to it for me; I'd never make a drawing which animated into another drawing – that's something that I've never done. So I just animated a whole bunch of drawings and then we shot them in three sittings – Paul and I did it together, because it was more fun, and for three evenings we put the sound down and shot it from beginning to end. I'd made it after my assessment and I showed it for the first time at the final show.

I got it into the Whitechapel Open in 1994, having left college in 1993. And then I saw an advert for submissions for this programme called *Slacker Attitude* at London Electronic Arts. I sent a tape to the curator George Barber, and it got selected. It was in a programme with John Baldessari and Bruce Nauman and stuff like that, and I thought: 'This is good.'

MS: *So you were immediately being connected to other artists who you thought were interesting?*

AC: Yes, I thought it was amazing. It was at the ICA and so on. But then I didn't make any films for ages because I thought that I would get pigeon-holed into making animations, so I didn't make another one for about seven years – I was just doing drawings.

In 1999, Angela Kingston put *Ann(i)Mated* into an exhibition called *Girl* at Angel Row Gallery in Nottingham. In the same year I made one with flickering ink blots called *Untitled (Night Beast)* (1999) and one with stills called *Me* (1999). Then in 2000 I made five more films, three with Paul which were made in about nine days, when we had access to some equipment.

MS: *And that's when you applied to animate!?*

AC: Yes, we got the commission for *Rotting Artist* in 2001. When we got the commission, we found it quite difficult to get over the idea that *Rotting Artist* was going to be on television. We'd never thought anybody was going to look at the work we made previously, as we were just making it because it was interesting to do and quite good fun. But with this one we just found it difficult to get over that idea – that somebody was going to be looking at it on the television, it seemed a bit invasive…

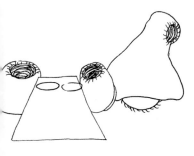

Ann(i)Mated Ann Course (1999)/49

MS: *So were you happy with the end result?*

AC: Not entirely. Partly because of the music, which is Beethoven's Ninth – we chose it because of the association with *A Clockwork Orange*. But I don't think it was the right recording to choose. I like the drawings, some of them, and I don't think it's bad, but I don't enjoy watching it. I think if I did it again, it would be different – it was my first commission.

MS: *You made other films around the same time, like* Black Magic *(2002)...*

AC: Yes, that was fun. The sound is really good, it's from *O Lucky Man* (1973) which I'd seen when the artist Mark Aerial Waller showed it. We bought the soundtrack for it and used it. The reason we called it *Black Magic* was that we just made it in about three hours and it was really good fun to put together, it seemed to just work.

MS: *Is there a pattern to how you work with music – does the sound always come first?*

AC: Yes, there might be particular images which I associate with the songs. When I made *Shit Belt* (2000), I chose the music from *The Great Escape* (1963), which is really particular because when I was a kid we'd watch it every Christmas, and I did have some ideas of images which would go with that. But it might only be one or two drawings, for instance, the rest are put in spontaneously at the time of shooting. Paul chose the music for *Hunt Me* (2004), whereas he wasn't interested at all in *The Great Escape* theme so I made that one on my own.

MS: *Do you think making more animations has changed the way you look at your drawings and sculptures?*

AC: I think I was deluded about the value of a drawing, basically. I drew for years and thought that I could do something, and I have done something with drawings in a way. But I thought that I could really do something with small drawings and I was very fussy about how they should be looked at, and how you shouldn't look at them with anything between you and them, like a piece of glass – they should be seen exactly as they were made. But it was really good groundwork – I did loads of groundwork and research,

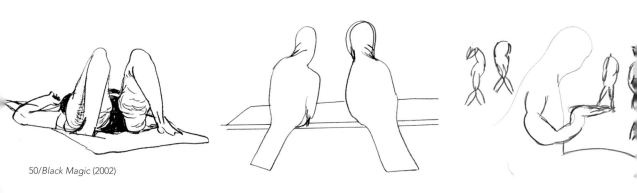

50/*Black Magic* (2002)

basically, and I have sourced loads of things from those drawings.

The fact that I've done quite well with the films is really what's made the difference, because it means that I can show an animation and I can get to show drawings and sculptures alongside the films – it's enabled me to do that, and given me confidence.

MS: *Do you think in terms of installation, where the animations and the drawings play off each other?*

AC: No, it's very difficult to think like that. I don't find it easy to think about things unless I'm actually doing them and I'm not particularly interested in successful exhibitions – I'm more interested in particular pieces of work and whether they're good or not, rather than thinking, 'That was a good show.' I don't really value that. However, you get certain opportunities and you make work to fit that, so that in turn shapes the work – but you don't want to make work in order to sell, that's the kiss of death.

It's a similar subject matter with the sculptures, but as three-dimensional objects, they almost have the before and after moment again, I think. I have a sculpture of these three pies which are different sizes, they're glazed pink and they say 'you', 'me' and 'them' – it's taken from the bunkers that are in *Rotting Artist*. But you do things with a pie, cut it open or cook it, so these other moments are implied…

MS: *The before and after element is like having these tiny little narratives embedded in the works, so that they are just one part of a process…*

AC: Yes, exactly. In *No Horizon*, a show at Firstsite in Colchester, I had a sculpture of a chimney brush sticking out of a chimney, which is also from *Rotting Artist*.

The films to me are quite quiet, small things and they come from quite quiet, small drawings. And I always struggled with the idea of actually saying something – why have I got the right to say something, why would anyone be interested? And being commissioned to make *Rotting Artist* made me much more confident about that. A commission like that is really important, because once you've done a commission and handled a budget and delivered it on time and proved that you can do it, then people know that they can trust you to do it again. And it's good to do something and to finish it for a deadline, knowing it will be shown, even if it's not totally successful – you learn from it.

MS: *So did being commissioned as an animator change the way you thought about yourself?*

AC: No, it worried me because people said I shouldn't do it if I wanted to get on in the art world – but then, people also told me that you shouldn't tell anyone that you studied illustration. And animation has become much more celebrated in the art world since 2001 – there's a lot more animation in galleries now – and perhaps I've benefited from that, I don't know.

I did associate animation with quite a negative thing, which is strange. If you were to ask me about food, why would I think of something that I don't want first of all? But somehow it's programmed in my brain like that, and it has to be somebody's fault! Whose fault is it?

MS: *Is it Uncle Walt?*

AC: No, I think it's the purists – people being purist about what animation is and not being more open about what it could be.

I'm interested in ceramics and I like to know about glazes and so on, but I don't want to spend a lifetime mastering one type of glaze – no thanks. But is there a big difference between ceramics and animation? With ceramics, people immediately just think of pots, but it's much broader than that. It's the same with animation.

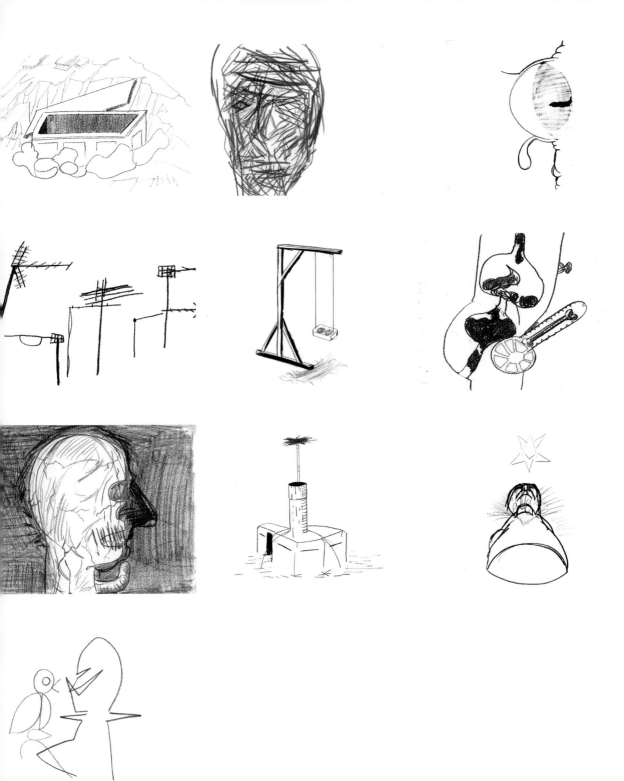

Inger Lise Hansen

Inger Lise Hansen studied Fine Art at North East London Polytechnic, St Martins College of Art and San Francisco Art Institute. Working with film, she has investigated the possibilities of time-lapse and stop-motion photography to animate landscapes and architecture. Her films, including Hus *(1998), which shows the accelerated decay of a house, and* Adrift *(2004), a portrait of the Arctic island of Spitzbergen, have won prizes at film festivals around the world. Based in both Norway and London, she continues to make films as well as teach.*

She is currently working on Proximity, *her first film for* animate!, *which explores Scandinavian landscapes from unexpected and somewhat disorienting perspectives.*

MS: *What was your background?*

IH: I started working with film when I was at art college. On my foundation course there was somebody who suggested I should try film because there was a lot of movement in my drawings, they were almost running off the page. But then I didn't really think about it until I was at the North East London Polytechnic, where there was a film department. They suggested that I stayed in the painting department, but I was starting to use a Super 8 camera with drawings and objects, and I've been working with 16mm film since then, animating things…

MS: *When you were first working with film, did you think of yourself as being an animator?*

IH: Not at all, no – I still find it difficult! Because there was a combination of moving drawings and sculpture. And I was more interested in the real world, and interacting with it. I was also doing a lot of photography at the same time. It was more and more about interacting with the real world using surreal documentations – a way of observing and examining objects or architecture or landscape. That process is also about time, I think – building time or constructing time, which is the animation element. I'm not really interested in animation as such, but I'm interested working out what time is and constructing another time.

MS: *When you first started out, who were your influences?*

IH: One of them was Jan Svankmajer. I saw his work quite early, and also the Quay Brothers. I even went and worked in Svankmajer's old studio in Prague for a year, observing and seeing how they moved puppets and constructed scenes. It was after the Velvet Revolution, so I was there when the studios were hardly running at all, there was just one film they were producing for Austrian television, but they were keeping it ticking over. From being a state studio, they turned it into a production company, but all the techniques and the skills were there, so I was working with the animator from Svankmajer's films and also his cameraman, learning lots of tricks about how to set things up. It was very studio-based animation, puppet animation. Something that's been very useful to me. But while I was sitting there watching all this stuff, I also felt, 'I need to get out of here, I want to do my own things!' And I really couldn't see myself being part of any studio, I had to do something that was completely constructed by myself.

That's also to do with my background from London, and San Francisco where I did my MA in Filmmaking at the Art Institute, which was all based around experimental film and felt closer to me than the European animation.

MS: *Lawrence Jordan, the animator, was one of the people who taught you in San Francisco – was he a big influence?*

IH: He was always very interested in my films and very supportive and I do find his films very interesting, even though I work in a completely different way. But the strange moods and eerie qualities of his work, and its precision, are very interesting. Ernie Gehr was also my advisor there, and structuralist film, or whatever you want to call it, was also quite interesting, although I've always worked against it in a way. It was more interesting for me to think of film as an organic structure, as it comes out of an intuitive process, rather than imposing a rigid structure beforehand. I was quite frustrated with structuralist film to begin with but now it has become an important reference, although I think my earlier work especially is a kind of organised chaos.

The Quay Brothers and Svankmajer are the most obvious references for stop-motion film animators and I think they make fantastic films, but I find that I'm left wondering more about someone like Rachel Whiteread's work – how she makes empty space solid, into a negative of the original structure. Or Gordon Matta-Clark, it's very poetic the way his work challenges the functions and physical limitations of architecture.

MS: In terms of the way your own films have developed, do you think there's a common thread then?

IH: I think each film is like a whole thing in itself, like a whole world, because I take a long time making each one. Each one is quite a separate project, even though if I look at them all together there are recurring techniques and themes. They're also quite chronological, so there's something I find out through making one film which will go on to the next, because my work is often open-ended. I usually have a plan at the beginning, which goes through a whole set of different stages and considerations.

The technique of working frame-by-frame, and working on film as well, are quite good structuring elements for me – these practical limitations allow for a more free process to go on *within* each film. I might have a lot of ideas of what it will look like at the beginning and there are always a lot of routes I might take, but then I have to narrow it down and cut away. And when I cut away, sometimes what's left is quite simple in the end but it might appear quite structured or organised.

MS: *Does that kind of development happen while you're shooting, or at the editing stage?*

IH: I think both – and the same with the sound. Each film is different. With *Hus* I did the shooting separately from the sound, even though I was using bits of the sound from the location, and it was just one shoot. But the other films were put together over a long period of time, shots are put in and taken out, and in that sense I'm not very economical – I make few films and I could probably make more if I was a bit more economical! But it seems important to have this process, *to get to something.*

That's happening very much in my new animate! film, *Proximity,* too. For a while, I've been experimenting with turning the camera upside down. That started with *Adrift* for a very particular reason. I was in Spitzbergen near the North Pole in a landscape without any references like trees or houses. I couldn't make sense of it, I couldn't judge scale or distance at all, and sometimes, depending on the weather, it even looked like it was upside down. It was like my own eyes were playing tricks, and that was very interesting to me. Also, it was interesting to fix the camera upside down – that's a whole new area for me, the perspective. I'm always interested in some kind of disorientation. Earlier it was the subject in front of the camera, the architecture or whatever, which was manipulated or displaced in some way, but now it is the camera itself. In some ways the films are all

56/*Proximity* (concept & production stills) Inger Lise Hansen (2006)

about the same thing, about *wanting* to be disorientated and wondering about what is real and not real. You want to get lost…

MS: *Because it's only when you're lost that you can see things afresh?*

IH: Exactly. Again, I think the framework of making a film gives me that possibility, because within each film I get lost and I have to figure something out from there – and that's when things happen; I think that's very important. It takes a long time and it has a lot of technical stages to go through; it gives a solid frame to get lost in. With video, I just get lost immediately! I think video has its own special qualities, but for me the discipline of film and the length of the process are both very helpful in this area of getting lost and coming back.

With the animate! film, I had planned to do a lot of movement and to animate the landscape because in a way that's what I knew from before, and I wrote a proposal based on that. Then I discovered that when I'm animating things, it takes away from what's really happening in the image. I came to that conclusion from the experience of starting to work with it, which is a real relief at the same time – to let go of that. I don't always have to dig into the ground to make some sense of it, or to see it, or to know what it is. The construction can be just with the use of the camera. And that goes back very much to experimental film, something like Ernie Gehr's *Side/Walk/Shuttle* (1991) with all these different perspectives and the camera moving in a lift and buildings behind shooting up. It's really disorientating, purely from the movement of the camera and the perspective. That's a kind of animation too. That's something that I learnt in Prague, to do all these things – tilts and tracks and so on – in animation.

MS: *Does it make a difference too that this film is being made for television?*

IH: I've thought a lot about it in terms of looking at it on a small screen and what that does – I find that interesting. It's interesting too that a lot of people are going to see it at the same time, in different places, different environments – that's a great form of multiple-screen installation! And then I can also continue working on it to make a film. There will be different versions. The one for animate! will be three minutes and I'm hoping to keep that quite simple, and then I want to make a longer version which will include more locations.

At the moment I'm shooting in Norway and Denmark, and I've found it's necessary to have a very flat landscape with straight horizons. When you look at it the right way up, it just looks like you're travelling along a beach, but when you turn it over it becomes a mysterious space – you recognise the elements, the sand and the stones, but you don't know where you are situated as a viewer.

MS: *Like in* Adrift, *when the rock pools are draining but the water is draining horizontally because of how it is framed…*

IH: Yes, but this is more minimal than that in a way. In *Adrift*, there were so many complex things going on in each shot, with the tide and the corresponding animation. I also had to find areas with several levels of different heights, so I could animate something in the foreground and then something nearer to the sea, so it was quite complicated to find the right spots.

For the new film it has to be flat, and the surface is important. What's nearest to the camera is at the top of the frame. In a way it's coming very much from what I discovered in *Adrift* with the perspectives, but it's much simpler.

MS: *With the other films, like* Hus *and* Adrift, *the manipulation in front of the camera suggests these processes of decay, which is perhaps another connection with Svankmajer – the uncanniness of seeing an apparently natural process of decay compressed into a short space of time.*

IH: I was interested in imitating a natural process, to see how close I could get to imitate something that will happen over millions of years. For a house to crumble, as it does in *Hus*, it would take a long time.

MS: *But you also wanted to show that it was illusion, so you show the passing of a single day with the shadows, or people appearing in some of the shots…*

IH: Yes, there are lots of people in the shots, and there are also cables and strings. In *Hus*, I kept all that stuff in – that was important, the whole idea of construction, of *constructing* an illusion and having the essence of that illusion visible. The whole thing was about construction, the construction of the deconstruction, and film itself as a

construction, something that you make from nothing.

MS: *I guess that reflects back a bit to those structural-materialist filmmakers.*

IH: Yes, very much so. Although, at the same time, for me *Hus* was also a kind of documentary, because when I was in California I would see all these abandoned houses everywhere, from when people had said, 'Let's go here and see if we can find some gold', and then when there was nothing they would just leave and go somewhere else. There are all these places sitting around that nobody cares about. It was also very much about the place and the temporary feeling of Californian houses – everything feels like that there.

MS: *Have you shown your work much in documentary contexts?*

IH: Not much – it's more been an art context, or experimental film. But the documentary element is important for me. More and more that's an element I'm becoming aware of. I think documentary is about one's own relationship to the world, it's not about any kind of 'truth' – it's always a kind of personal observation. A few people have said to me here in Norway that my films should be discussed in the context of documentary films, because they would raise that question. I tell my own truth through this obvious construction, in the real world.

MS: *Do you know how you would define animation then? People sometimes think of it quite narrowly, but you give the sense that your understanding of it is much broader.*

IH: To animate means to bring to life and for me this is a way to give a piece of the real world a different kind of life and to interrogate it. It gives the landscape a different and accelerated time, and questions what is real and not real. With this I am reviewing and reinventing natural processes, while also pointing to the frame-by-frame construction and building of time itself.

About my latest film, *Proximity,* I think it's constructing another *place* – not just another cinematic time and space. It feels like *somewhere;* another reality and that gives narrative associations.

MS: *What else are you working on?*

IH: I'm working on a public art piece in my home town in Norway, which is related to a big Gothic cathedral. A big glass visitors' centre is being built next to it and I have a commission to make a permanent video installation. So I'm trying to work out if I will do something on lots of different screens, or one screen, and how it will work in this glass building. It's quite a challenge, because it's such a contradiction, to make something that is non-permanent and time-based into something permanent. The church itself is very interesting, it's one thousand years old and it's been built in lots of different stages, it's been burnt down and rebuilt, and the most recent sculptures were added in the 1980s.

MS: *So the building you see is really a tiny part of this composite building, which has existed over hundreds of years?*

IH: Yes, you can see the old and the new next to each other – it's a visual disharmony, but it's really beautiful. And it's also a challenge to approach something like that, such a huge dominating building – I think I will have to do something very intimate and simple.

Proximity Inger Lise Hansen (2006)/61

Jonathan Hodgson

Jonathan Hodgson was born in Oxford in 1960 and educated at Liverpool Polytechnic and the Royal College of Art. His animations, which employ a restless variety of styles, have won many awards including a BAFTA for The Man With the Beautiful Eyes *(1999). Having worked for other animation studios he set up the production company Sherbet with Jonathan Bairstow in 1996, through which he has also produced high profile commercial work.*

His first animate! film was Feeling My Way *(1997), which portrayed a journey from home to work through the filter of the walker's free associations.* Camouflage *(2001), his second commission, was an exploration of the impact of mental ill-health on the person's family and friends, drawn from his personal experience.*

MS: *How did you come to animation?*

JH: I didn't really have any intention of doing animation to start off with. I went into illustration and it was only when I did my degree course that I got into animation, really as an excuse – I wanted to change courses because I didn't like the course I was on at Brighton, and some of my friends who I'd done foundation with had gone up to Liverpool and seemed to be having a better time socially, which seemed to be the most important thing at the time! The only course that they had at Liverpool that they didn't have at Brighton was animation, so I threw together a portfolio of storyboards and things like that and said that I wanted to do animation. So they let me come up.

Ray Fields ran the animation course at Liverpool, who was, and still is, an inspirational character: a combination of maverick artist and drill sergeant. He was quite frightening at first, but he was very anti-establishment, which I liked and he was certainly very anti the animation industry as it was then. He tried to get students to find an alternative way of working, to shake off the bad influences from mass culture and to find a more personal way of working. His big thing was *colour*, but one of the most interesting things for me was being encouraged to work in a very spontaneous way and to look at artists who worked in that way – semi-abstract with quite minimal lines – Matisse is obviously one of them, but also Roger Hilton and Terry Frost who were associated with the St Ives School. Ray Fields had a shack down near St Ives and there was quite a strong influence from the more abstract of the St Ives artists.

There was also a very strong observational component – I think that's where the documentary element came from in my work – although a lot of my work has always been observational. Even when I was at school, I used to do cartoons based around people at the school and my mates. Nothing I've ever done has really been based on escapism, it's always been about life.

MS: *Did filmmakers influence you at this point, or was it more fine artists?*

JH: It was definitely more fine art. The kind of films I liked were those early 60s kitchen sink films, *Saturday Night and Sunday Morning* (1960) and that kind of thing. I don't know how it tied in with what I was doing in animation, but it was looking at ordinary people, rather than science fiction or something – trivial things, but in a way profound. Over the years as I've started to think more about what I'm doing and why, it has been a fascination with small unimportant things which have something quite meaningful in them.

MS: *So what happened when you left college?*

JH: I did a postgraduate course at the Royal College of Art and I was kind of geared up to try to work as an animator. I suppose my plan when I left college was just to make films and get work at animation studios to make money, and it's more or less like that still. I do a bit of commercial work, get a bit of money and get a bit of time, and carry on doing my own stuff.

MS: *You've talked about keeping quite a strict separation between your commercial work and your personal work…*

JH: Yes, working in advertising can be great, but it can also be a bit undermining as well. You hardly ever run into anyone from an agency that understands what you're trying to do and, even if they do, they're still beholden to their clients and there are so many layers of people involved. Through trial and error, I've found that what I can do is work with other people and oversee the job and make sure that everything works properly and that we're doing what the client wants. But it's not very much to do with me, it's more to do with diplomacy and understanding a bit about the technical side.

MS: *Both your animate! films feel very personal. Could you talk about how* Feeling My Way *started out?*

JH: Almost since I first came to London I'd had the idea of making a film about some aspects of my experience of London. I'd made this nightclub film in Liverpool, which was very much about the social life in Liverpool and going to clubs, being slightly on the periphery of things. That had worked quite well, and the thing in London is that you're even more on your own, it's even more of a lonely place, and it's possible to go for days without even speaking to anyone.

I wanted to make a film about London where you're viewing it from behind a screen which is inside your head, conscious of what's around you but only interacting on a cerebral level and not speaking to people. But it took me ages to come up with the idea of making a film about just walking to work. It came to me because I used to do that walk every day and after a year of doing that walk I thought, 'This is my experience of London, this encapsulates lots of aspects of it.' It's something that is so trivial and commonplace, and most people wouldn't even think it was a worthy subject for a film, and from the moment I had the idea I knew exactly what to do with the film. I knew I had to make a live action film and find a way to draw on top of it.

MS: *Was that the first time that you'd combined live action and animation?*

JH: Yes, it was. I had worked with live action on earlier films, I used to shoot Super 8 for reference before I had access to video and then use one of those Super 8 viewers, advancing through single frames and using it as a guide to sketch the next position in the drawing. So the movement in a lot of my early stuff is quite accurate, because it is derived from live action. But I'd never married the two on the same screen.

I got a lot of help from Dick Arnall because I'd never worked with a computer before and he persuaded me to try. It was about 10 years ago and computers weren't anywhere near as advanced as they are now. I actually ended up buying this Amiga computer, which was mainly used for games but it was quite good for animation. There was some animation software you could use, but I didn't use any of that in the end, I just used it as a way of digitising the live action which was shot on Hi8 video. I digitised the footage

64/Feeling My Way Jonathan Hodgson (1997)

and then roughly edited it – it was clunky editing, linear, and when you cut one frame out you had to wait for the whole timeline to reset.

It took a long time to edit it, and the worst thing was printing the frames out onto paper, because I'd come out of the digital domain where you print the frames onto inkjet paper. I would print out a whole sequence and do whatever I wanted to do on top of it, and then actually shot those frames again onto 35mm film. I digitised every other frame, so it's like looking at live action but with only 12.5 images per second, which actually helps to marry the animated quality of the drawings with live action – the photographs look less like video because they're a bit jerkier.

Shooting the video was quite quick and then there was this huge chunk of time when I was mostly printing out stuff, and then a bit at the end when I was actually doing the animation.

MS: *With* Feeling My Way, *and with some of your other work, it feels like an attempt to allow film access to inner space, to open it up to a kind of experience which novels can address but which films normally cannot.*

JH: I'm not a great writer, in terms of scripts, and that's why I've used that vaguely documentary format while still wanting to bring something personal into that. And I've always thought that animation was quite a good way of expressing abstract thoughts, another layer of information around a live action element. With *Feeling My Way*, the images almost looked like thoughts and most people who've seen it say that – not only did they feel that they were in my head, but they were also identifying with those thoughts. A lot of the time those thoughts are not easy to write down, if you write it down it can seem more significant than it really is, but as animations they're just there and then they're gone.

I like the idea that you get to a certain point in the journey and something's triggered in your head and you think the same thought each time – it might not have much of an association with what you're seeing, but it's just that for some reason you thought it on one particular day, and then each successive day you're reminded that you thought of it the last time you were there. It's about the overlooked things that we all experience, that are part of the human condition but they're not things that you can bring into conversation a lot of the time, they wouldn't be worth mentioning.

MS: Camouflage *is more explicitly personal, in that it's partly autobiographical. Can you talk about how that project started?*

JH: Around the time that I had the idea of making the film, I'd had a bit of therapy and a lot of stuff about my childhood had come up through that. My thought was to make a film about aspects of my childhood that, as a child, are not discussed with anybody and are kept quite secret.

My mum had schizophrenia, and as kids we felt very isolated and embarrassed and didn't want anyone to know about it. It was only later in life that we could talk about it without it feeling really uncomfortable – it still makes me feel quite uncomfortable, but I suppose I'd come to the point in my life where I was ready to express that. It was the idea that a lot of the time with mental illness, the focus is on the person who is ill, but not on the people that are around them. I was also interested in the idea that as a child you look to your parents for guidance and that what they tell you is how you make sense of the world, so if your parents are saying something that's obviously at odds with what you can see, it can be pretty confusing. For quite a long time my mum said odd things that I believed and it was only later that I realised that they were just things that were connected with her illness.

One of the reasons that I got other people involved and got them to tell their stories was because it was all so explicit and personal, and out of respect for my mother I wasn't actually ready to say everything that was in my mind. I really wanted someone else to say it for me – I didn't want to say, 'This is a film about me and my mum.' And since making the film I've met a surprising number of people who've had a similar experience.

MS: Camouflage *uses lots of different visual styles, and you make quite explicit choices about changing the style and the points of reference for each person's story.*

JH: Part of that is because I don't see myself as a designer, because I could never work in a consistent style – it's always going off in different directions. So I feel more comfortable trying to use different styles all the time. Also, I wanted the people who were involved in the film, the people who I'd interviewed, to do some drawings. I persuaded them to draw, even though they said they couldn't, because I think even when people say they can't draw they can usually do something quite interesting, especially if it's to do with some-thing quite personal.

I didn't copy their styles as such, but I tried to use elements of them and to give each interview its own flavour, while keeping the drawings not too sophisticated. I'm not that into refined styles or slickness, I like raw drawings and quite clunky movements. Certainly for this kind of subject matter I think it's more suited to something a bit raw and ham-fisted, which is how I communicate really – I'm not the most articulate person – so a lot of the drawing probably feels a bit like that too. There's a bit of me that feels like I'm selling out if I try to make things too refined and slick.

MS: *But you also juxtapose those fully animated sequences with some live action sequences, involving actors. Was that a departure for you too?*

JH: Yes, I hadn't really done anything with actors before and it was quite a big leap. It actually became much more involved than I'd wanted it to be, because my original idea was to just shoot it with a video camera or Super 8 and just do it myself, but then I got a live action producer involved and she'd got a crew together. Suddenly I had to be the director, working with these lighting rigs and so on, and I was really not prepared for it and found it slightly overwhelming. But those live action sequences were quite necessary, because there were certain things you couldn't do with the animation. Sometimes if you look at a photographic image, you can just tell something from somebody's eyes which can communicate quite a lot, or just a tiny gesture, and those very subtle emotional things are not very easy to get across in animation. That's why I wanted to balance the animation, which was very much about these raw feelings and this build-up of pressure in your head, with the live action stuff. The little girl who played the main character was very calm and still-looking, and I wanted to get across this idea that there was all this stuff going on inside [her head] and that she was holding herself together, being very composed.

MS: *What do you think of the animation scene in general at the moment?*

JH: A lot of it doesn't interest me, a lot of it never did interest me that much. I've always looked to other media for inspiration, I hardly ever look at animation and see something exciting.

It's quite a strange time in animation at the moment, because everything's blending in so much – there's so much more digital work going into live action and animation is

going the same way, using digital compositing. Whether you're an animation or a live action director now, you're using the same equipment and tools – After Effects, Final Cut Pro, Photoshop and so on. But I do find that my brain works in a different way when I'm using all that equipment. I can't listen to music when I work with it, because I have to think much harder about the technical side all the time. I don't know if that will get easier, but it's not the same way that I used to work – I used to do a lot of drawings and be thinking of something else while I was doing them, and I think that's changed the way I make films. I feel that I haven't quite found where I'm going with the new technology yet.

Animation has changed so much in the last few years because there are so many people who have grown up with computers, people like the guys from Shynola who do amazing CGI for pop videos. Technically it's way beyond anything I could conceive of doing. But I think that a lot of it is about the surface now, the main thing seems to be about how things look, and I still come back to, 'What are you trying to say?'

I'd rather not think of myself as an animator, really, because I hate being pigeon-holed and I've never got that much inspiration from animation anyway – it was just the area that I ended up working in. It can be a bit of a ghetto and a lot of animators I've met have no interest in art or in any culture outside of animation. There's a preconceived idea about what animation is and there are the frequently asked questions about animation, which are always the same – Disney, computer animation, *Wallace and Gromit*, etc – and they're never very much to do with what I do.

Action : Walking past a church, thoughts
        about the day ahead.

Tim Hope

Tim Hope took a degree in theology and worked as a stand up comedian before making his first animated short The Wolfman *(1999), which won the McLaren Animation Prize at Edinburgh International Film Festival in 2000. A self-taught animator, he joined Passion Pictures in 2000 and is now an acclaimed director of commercials and music videos, having collaborated with REM and Coldplay amongst others.*

His animate! film Minema Cinema *(2004), emulating a creative process developed by London's Scene & Heard theatre group, used cutting edge computer animation to realise three short scripts by children.*

MS: Minema Cinema *was a very unusual production – could you talk about how it came about?*

TH: It was inspired by Scene & Heard theatre group, which is based in London. I'd been to see their shows a few times. They get children aged seven upwards to write stories and the stories are very unprocessed – they don't edit them for moral content or anything. Then adult actors perform the scripts and they take them as seriously as they can. Basically it creates an amazing form of theatre which is just so free and ridiculous and moving, with stories about vacuum cleaners that fall in love with the moon and things like that. They don't edit them, but it's a very sophisticated structure at the same time – they do encourage the children to put a structure into their stories and to get things moving forward.

Scene & Heard get them to work with non-human characters partly because it opens up the children's imaginations and takes it into a different world, as they'd found that when children are asked to write about human characters they often just write, 'I got up in the morning and I went to the shops' and so on. It makes fascinating theatre, and I thought we should have a go at making it into an animated film, to see what happens. All I was trying to do was to translate the spirit of that to an animation environment, to be true to what the children were trying to say, even if they weren't trying to say anything! And all of the children I worked with had done the course before.

MS: *Was it important that there would be more than one story?*

TH: Yes, although it was a nightmare doing that because of the amount of work involved. Being based on the theatre shows, it had to be about the concept rather than just one child's voice.

MS: *What was the process of working with the children?*

TH: Scene & Heard nominated the three children: Kevin Pinto, Thomas Gwyther and Acai Duang Arop, and we just went to work. We didn't vet the scripts in any way, we just sat down with them and worked through the ideas.

MS: *Did they have strong preconceptions about what an animation should be?*

TH: Well strangely, they found it quite liberating, relative to the theatre experience. They don't see any theatre normally, so it was a lot easier for them to connect with films and animation. Obviously their associations were to do with *Shrek* (2001) and that kind of thing, which to a certain extent I didn't want to fight too much. I didn't mind that they had a mainstream perception – I'd quite happily have gone down as mainstream a visual look as they wanted. But it was a tight balance and I'm not sure if the final product is for children. It was never supposed to be screened at children's film festivals, although it has been a bit. The worlds that they create are probably more interesting for adults.

MS: *So you storyboarded the films from their scripts?*

TH: They spent a couple of days working on the script and we read it through, just to see if there was any way we could help them. There was a little bit of editing, but there was very little leading of what they were doing – we might have said, 'try again'. So then we got storyboard artists in to draw their characters and they found that very easy to work with – is he happy, is he tall and so on – and they had great fun bringing these characters to life.

Kevin could actually draw a bit himself, so he invented the idea of a cactus being in a pot with legs sticking out of the bottom – he pretty much drew the silhouettes of what most of the characters would look like. And Thomas knew that he wanted the face of

Blossom the blouse to be in the middle. They all had quite strong ideas. I don't think the children were very different from how I am when I'm working with a storyboard artist, it's quite a simple way of communicating.

MS: *What did they think of the final films?*

TH: I'm not really sure. They definitely enjoyed it – it was a great experience for them. The screening at Channel 4 was quite a big thing, whereas with the theatre show there are 10 plays at the same time and there is less focus on each child, it's more of a group event. We were aware that the films were more focused on each individual child, which wasn't exactly what we wanted to do, and such a huge amount of work had gone into each one that it was slightly disproportionate. But I think they got a lot out of it.

MS: *Your own background is in performance?*

TH: Yes, I did a bit of stand up comedy on the London circuit, I was doing writing and performance and multi-media stuff. I'd created this thing called The Pod, which was a techno act parodying The Shamen and The Orb. That's how I got into doing computer graphics, because I was doing parody computer graphics for the visuals for The Pod.
    I didn't have an art school or film school background at all, and animation is good in that it's quite inclusive. I started out doing performance with animation behind me, and I realised that computer animation is both really easy and really powerful. I started doing it around 1997 and I realised there's a lot more that you can do with it than the conventional computer generated stuff that people were doing at the time. I realised you could just take photos of stuff and cut them out and stick them into a computer generated world. So I just spotted that this was quite an exciting place to be and that it was actually quicker to make little short films than it was to make bits of performance and put on a show, because for that you have to organise a venue and send out press releases and so on.

MS: *So how did you first show your films?*

TH: The first one I really made was *The Wolfman*. I sent it to the Edinburgh Film Festival and it won best animation film, so I thought, 'OK, I am an animator now!'

MS: *Had you thought of yourself as an animator up to that point?*

TH: No, I thought of myself as a performer with animation behind me. I'd do these gigs, performing in front of these animated worlds and people would come up afterwards and say, 'Oh, I really liked the animation.' I became aware that I was only going to go so far as a performer and at first I really resented that people liked the animation more than [they liked] me! But eventually I thought this was something I was good at and that I should focus on it.

MS: *I read that you were against people being trained as animators and that you felt it was important you'd been self-taught…*

TH: Yes, I do tend to say things like that… I don't know if I am opposed to it in any way; I was very arrogant in my time.
   I think anyone just turning up in a discipline can be handicapped, or they can just be unleashed and find themselves. I was about 27 and I had all these ideas, and suddenly I was able to do all these things with computer animation and I realised that I could get a lot of these ideas onto the screen. Instantly I just found it very liberating and it unleashed all these visual ideas – I had no visual ideas before that, but suddenly I was being forced to develop a visual imagination. Computer animation does unleash a lot people – all you need is a computer and you can make a film in your bedroom, which is very exciting because it's not based on having a certain background or training. But five years later, I'm not sure it's made that much difference. I was proud not to have gone to college and just to have discovered it myself, but I have realised that it takes time and skill and I've had to learn a hell of a lot – I think loads of great stuff comes out of art colleges.

MS: *You've also said that computer animation is a communication tool and a way of immediately connecting with people, whereas animation previously had been something of a shut-off, self-contained world…*

TH: I think that is true. I think spending 12 months on two minutes of animation… some amazing stuff has been done like that and I wouldn't want to dismiss it… but I think a lot of people would find it very hard to work like that – most people would find that horrendous. And anyone who's a writer and wants to write things and get loads of ideas

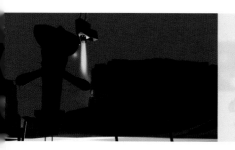

across would find it torture.

I think it is quite a dangerous mindset, the animation mindset – speaking as someone who has spent five years peering slightly myopically at a computer. *Minema Cinema* took nine months, which even though it's a 20-minute animation is quite a long time, and it's mind numbing as well, because even though you've had a few ideas, on the whole it's just a slog. Computer animation can just speed it all up.

MS: *Are you more interested in animation where it's fused with live action then, or where there's some crossover?*

TH: I think that's my aesthetic. It actually doesn't come across in *Minema Cinema* which is one of the more conventional things I've done visually, but my aesthetic was always about seeing what computer animation could do, mixing up live action and animation. I never liked computer generated surfaces and lit computer surfaces, and from the beginning I've worked with photographs and projected real world textures and models, rearranging them and using the computer as a way of realigning those elements and bits of video. So it's almost like building a whole set and then redoing it in the computer and seeing what that gives you.

I think computer animation is great as a story-telling structure, but visually at the moment it's not desperately exciting. There are some amazing pop videos, and the film *City Paradise* (2004), for example, is beautiful, a great combination of live action with computer generated images. I'm just not sure what's to be done with computer animation; now I feel much more interested in conventional animation. I think we're more aware now of the ease with which you can make computer animation and the shortcuts and the speed of it. It's still visually exciting, but I'm aware that it's losing something – I think it's going to be about making stuff by hand again and then editing and doing the sound in computers. That's what I feel at the moment. For me, it was always a combination of the fact that computers were so interesting and new and yet I always wanted to look back and combine them with the most handmade, clumsy traditional style – a kind of sentimental association with European animation, combined with computer animation which is so glittery.

I don't watch a huge amount of animation, partly just to try to avoid being in that world, to get my influences from other things and bring those in…

MS: *Who has influenced you?*

TH: At first it was very much the great art world animators of the 1970s and 80s – Jan Svankmajer and Yuri Norstein and the Russian animators – mixed in with other films and videos. I liked animation, but I also liked the realness of just filming something and bringing that into the world. That was always what I was playing with – is it a film or is it animation – and just mixing those two up. That was always the thing I found most exciting, not being sure if it's an animated world or a real world. And Michel Gondry has also been a massive influence.

MS: *It sounds like, as with Gondry, you don't keep a rigorous divide between your commercial work and your personal work – you feel your commercial work can be equally creative.*

TH: I do try to make interesting professional work and some of the pop videos have been quite interesting, and usually I'm given the chance to do something. They are asking me to come up with something and play around – with the Hewlett-Packard ads they were just saying to come up with something and to make it exciting. So I was being given these great opportunities, presumably because of people like Gondry and Spike Jonze, who've done exciting commercial work.

At the moment I'm working on this television show *The Mighty Boosh*, doing the visuals for that, the set design and the whole look of it, which I'm excited about. I'm trying to focus on stories and performance, working on scripts and narrative-driven stuff. Visual experimentation is always a secondary thing for me. You have to do it in pop videos and commercials, that's what I was being asked to do, but once you're dealing with narratives then you've got to focus on the story and then if you can bring a good look to it, that's great, but it's not the focus.

MS: *Do you still think of yourself as an animator?*

TH: Not really, no. Animation is a very exciting way to create quite strong vivid worlds, but I'm just learning at the moment and I'm moving towards film slowly. I think animation will inform that, it's taught me about lighting and camera angles and storyboarding and how to do all that stuff, but it hasn't necessarily taught me how to make an interesting film.

MS: *Having come to it from the outside, do you feel you could define animation?*

TH: I think it's possibly quite simple, that it's an individual's view of the world. Film is on the whole collaborative and the central collaboration is between the director and the actors – no good film is just one person's view. The actors and the script should, in a way, be more important than the director, and the director should be almost trying to make themselves invisible. Which is possibly true with animation too, but animation is one person's view – it's closer to writing a book or something. So animators possibly have quite a strong claim to be artists, more than film directors [do]. And that's the weakness of animators, they tend to be slightly self-absorbed and slightly lacking in range – even the great animators can have a slightly limited palette. Animation is more about one person's view, a completely created world – and I know that's not true and that there are lots of films that break the rule, but I think that describes the 'art' animator anyway.

The reason I think of it like that is because I'm conscious of my limitations and what I've been battling with, which is that as an animator I've realised that I'm stuck in my own head all the time. I don't think it's a bad thing, I think it's what makes it such an interesting and vivid world. To some extent, *Minema Cinema* was a desperate attempt to break away from having to look inside my own head for inspiration all the time – more than anything, I wanted it to be their world and [for me] to be as invisible as possible.

I was conscious that the look of *Minema Cinema* was quite mainstream – it's got animated characters with lip sync, it's very cartoony. I thought that would be an interesting thing to do in the context of animate! because I knew it wanted to avoid narrative-driven character animation stuff – I was quite keen to see how this fitted in, as a visually quite conservative but conceptually interesting piece. I knew it was going slightly against the grain of animate! but I wanted the film to be watchable by kids. I was aware I could just go for something very weird and take their stories into a world which was quite disturbing, but I think that would have been too obvious, trying to warp a child's world and make it weird and adulty. I wanted it to be more celebratory and for the children to feel like they'd made it, rather than for us to manipulate them. In the end, this just felt like the world they would be comfortable with – it's about them having something they could be proud of.

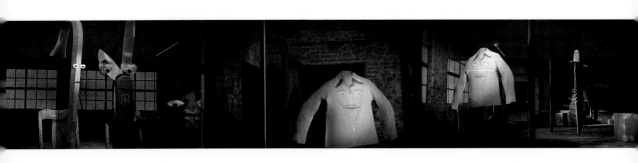

Ruth Lingford

Ruth Lingford worked for over a decade as an occupational therapist, before studying Fine Art & Art History at Middlesex University and Animation at the Royal College of Art. Working as a freelance animator since 1992, her films, which use a variety of computer animation techniques, won her immediate acclaim and several commissions, including the multi award-winning Pleasures of War *(1998), made for Channel 4. She teaches animation at both the Royal College and the National Film and Television School, and in 2005–06 spent a year teaching at Harvard University in the USA.*

Her first animate! film was What She Wants *(1994), a frank examination of sex and its commercialisation, showing a woman travelling on the underground who is plagued with fantasies. Her second commission,* The Old Fools *(2002), was an adaptation of a Philip Larkin poem, voiced by Bob Geldof.*

MS: *You came quite late to animation…*

RL: Yes, I was in my thirties. I was working as an occupational therapist and I'd had kids, and there came a point where I felt I wasn't as nice a person as all that, caring by day and then caring for the kids when I came home. Then two things happened. A friend of mine had a really bad car accident and nearly lost her life and her whole family. She said to me, 'If there's something you want to do just do it, because you never know what will happen tomorrow.' The other thing was that I was left some money by a tramp who had lived across the road and who I used to get a bit of shopping for now and again. He'd left me some money when he died, very unexpectedly, and it was enough for me to take a little break from my life.

I went back to do fine art at Middlesex University part time – I'd done a foundation course when I left school but I'd never really pursued it, because I didn't like the competitiveness. When the kids were small I did life drawing classes and when I was an occupational therapist I did some art therapy, so it was something I'd kept going a bit. I thought of it as a gap from my job, a bit of an indulgence, and certainly it wasn't anything I could imagine making a living from.

I was doing lots of painting and sculpture and etching, and then about halfway through the course I discovered animation almost by accident. I'd bought an old Standard 8 camera for five pounds on a stall and I was using it when I was painting, to record the development of my paintings. I had some film left, so I started experimenting, drawing and moving things about, and as soon as I got it back and watched it the scales fell from my eyes and I suddenly knew what I wanted to do when I grew up! So then I graduated from Middlesex in Animation and went on to the Royal College of Art to do a Masters in Animation.

MS: *So at this point, when you were starting out, what were your influences? Were they from animation, or were they from painting and fine art?*

RL: Mostly from painting probably. I was very influenced by Peter Webb, who taught art history when I was at Middlesex. He talked a lot about how artists have to deal with the difficult, dark stuff, that it was their duty and their right to deal with stuff that other people found unacceptable. Studying art history at Middlesex was a big influence, looking at a lot of paintings from the Renaissance onwards. So that all shows up in my work, there's a lot of stuff from painting and woodcuts.

My influences haven't really come from film at all, except for Jayne Parker. I saw her work quite early on and her early films are so beautiful, like *RX Recipe* (1980). She also did this really rough animation called *I Cat* (1980), which was very liberating to see, really simple and direct and visceral – it's about using animation as a weapon to get through people's defences.

MS: *What did you feel that you could do with animation, that you couldn't do with painting or something else? What was it that that attracted you to it so much?*

RL: The special thing, in the first work I did, is that it's about metamorphosis and how if you change one thing into another, other things happen on the way. It's a poetic juxtaposition of things that might not belong together, but then turn out to have some way of connecting. A lot of women do animation and there's a craft element to it – I used to be a knitter, and it's that patient process of working and then something beautiful coming out of it, something that you have total power and control over. It's quite a despotic feeling really, being an animator, and certainly at that stage in my life I wouldn't have had the confidence to direct actors, but I could make these drawings do whatever I wanted.

And just discovering what was in my unconscious as well, because when I started I was doing a lot of work that was absolutely straightforward stream of consciousness, I'd start drawing and I wouldn't know what was going to happen next at all. You'd look at your drawing and you'd discover what was in there, a mixture of accident and the unconscious mark-making, and then there's a feedback loop obviously, where you're looking at it and thinking about it and pushing it in one direction or another. That to me was a really interesting way of working, a kind of mediated stream of consciousness.

MS: *Had you made a lot of films before your first animate! film* What She Wants?

RL: No, that was my first film after the Royal College. The films I'd made at Middlesex were very much stream of consciousness – they were probably the most exciting things I've done, but full of animation clichés – and at the Royal College I was encouraged to plan and storyboard, although there were still bits of the films when I could just let things happen.

The influence on *What She Wants* was mainly from reading Michel Foucault's *History of Sexuality*. Where he talks about the relationship between sexuality and capitalism, and how capitalism stimulates us to sexualise ourselves and to experience ourselves as hypersexual beings with all these needs that have to be fulfilled. It was a bit of an essay film, in a way. It was my take on Foucault and then there's a lot of art history in there as well – Goya, Delacroix and so on. And it was also about, as an artist, having the right to mine your unconscious and that being useful stuff to get out there. So the film was a mixture of bits that were planned and bits that were just allowed to evolve.

MS: *Was the film a big success?*

RL: Yes, almost from the first time I did animation, I discovered that it gets you an audience, it gets you attention in a way that the static arts don't. What the animate! commission did was take me out of a world where I would have to do very incompetent inking and painting, as an animation drone, and it turned me into a director – obviously at a very low level, but it put me in a position of director, somebody with an individual voice. It also went to a lot of festivals, and took me with it.

MS: *It was also a relatively early use of computer animation…*

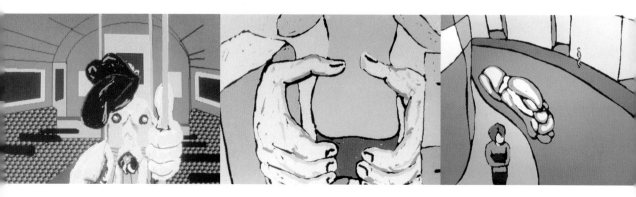

RL: That's right, and that also got some attention, because it was a funny time for computers. Computers were being used but when I was at the Royal College from 1990 to 1992, the animation department were hugely scornful of them – they thought there was no art in it. When I left college though I didn't have the choice, because I didn't have a rostrum camera and I couldn't do it any other way. I had an Amiga, which we had for the kids to play games on, and we invested in getting a whole megabyte of memory, which let me experiment with computer animation.

MS: *Were you comfortable with it, having come from this quite craft-based approach?*

RL: I was, and it also had the advantage in that I am very clumsy and I smudge things and knock things over. I'm quite messy on the computer, but at least it allowed me to be less messy. Also I found the limitations of that first animation – I didn't have many colours, and the pixels were huge – very good for my creative thinking. Now, when computers can do anything, it's more troublesome. Also, I seemed to be using the computer in the most logical way to get what I wanted, and it was quite a surprise to find I'd pioneered a technique that nobody knew was there.

It's still very much based on craft, because it's still your hand doing the drawing, and the look of it – particularly the black and white bits – has this look of linocut or woodcut. It does feel similar to printmaking, in that there's a gap between the original drawing and the finished product. Also just as with a linocut you get process marks, little marks from the bits of lino you haven't cut away, you get marks from the computer animation process which are quite similar, traces of the process.

MS: *And since then you've mixed computer animation with live action.*

RL: Yes, particularly in my second animate! film *The Old Fools*. It's really about enriching the image. I think Simon Pummell said you spend so long making an animated film, you want the audience to do a bit of work as well – you want it to be rich and layered and full of meaning, because it takes so long to do. Incorporating elements of live action is really an extension of the metamorphosis thing, where you're turning one thing into another – you're showing an image and then saying, 'But it's also like this, and like this', and making the audience reconcile these elements in their own minds.

MS: *You were talking about the importance of your work touching on taboos – was that important in* The Old Fools, *in the choice of the Larkin poem?*

RL: It was a very direct link to the Larkin poem. My daughter had borrowed a book of Larkin poems from the library and she read this one out at the dinner table, and it seemed quite shocking but also to beautifully mirror the experience we were having with my father, who became demented over a period of well over 10 years. Larkin wrote the poem when his mother was in a similar state I think, and it's a really beautiful, subtle portrayal of the mixture of emotions you feel. One of my Royal College films was about dementia as well, but from a less personal point of view – I'd worked a lot with people with dementia and it was based on that. But this was much more personal and I used images of my father's face in the film.

It was a softer film than I'd originally meant it to be, because it's a harsh subject – watching someone unravel is not a pretty sight, and I could have used much uglier images. I think I was somewhat constrained by respect for my father, and I think it's one of my more self-censored films, but people find it harsh enough I think.

MS: *Was it the first time you'd worked from a text like that?*

RL: It's the first time I'd done a poem, and that gave me lots of problems. It's a different sort of film than it would be if it weren't from a poem. The images in it are a lot less in-your-face than the other films.

Luckily, working on the computer I could have a guide voice-track to work to, and I'd do some animation and then immediately put it against the voice. What was obvious very quickly was that if you have something too fast or too strong happening visually, your ears switch off and it overpowers the poem. It was very important to me in this project that the poem was audible, because I wanted it to be a portrayal of the poem rather than my take on the subject, it wasn't like the poem was the starting point and I was riffing on it. For that reason, I didn't cut any of the poem and so it's quite crammed – it's a five and a half minute film and there's three minutes of reading in it, which is actually too much. People have said that they had to watch it a number of times to take it in, so it's a flawed film in that way, but I do think poetry and animation are a really good match, they have lots of stuff in common. What they have in common is the compression of the medium, they're very boiled down, very concentrated – the idea of

putting things together to make new thoughts and juxtaposing things that don't naturally go together to strike sparks.

They also have in common a very small audience! The interesting thing is that both animation and poetry can be funny or serious or anything in between, but poetry seems to have been painted into the serious corner and animation seems to have been painted into the funny corner, so I think there's great potential for them to help each other out of those pigeon-holes so they can cover more ground in the popular imagination.

MS: *You seem very clear about your identity as an animator, and very passionate about wanting to fight its corner and help it to define itself.*

RL: If people ask me what I do, I always say I'm an animator and I'm very proud to be an animator. It's such a new artform, there's so much unexplored territory and it's got enormous potential.

MS: *How would you define animation?*

RL: When I teach at the National Film and Television School I get asked this and they have a very wide definition of animation there – it's anything where the image is mediated frame-by-frame, which can include live action. But I think animation is about making the invisible visible, somehow, about making the impossible happen – that's the special quality that animation has, the idea that anything in your head can be communicated visually.

It's such a dizzying, vertiginously huge field and I think people respond to that vertigo by obsessively reinventing things and redoing things. It's always painful to see how people make the same films over and over again in an area where it's so easy to innovate, you hardly have to try at all to do something completely novel – originality is almost the default with animation, you almost have to try to not be original! To me the people that showed me the way were people like Yuri Norstein and Caroline Leaf, who are interested in animating in terms of depth, not just what can this image look like and how can we make different combinations of colour, but in terms of how can we mine deeper into human experience and the soul – unfashionable things like that.

MS: *So your definition is more about sensibility than technique…*

RL: Yes. Obviously technical definitions are important, but I'm interested in what it can do and how it can reflect human experience, how it communicates the subtlety and breadth of human experience – unconscious experience as well as conscious experience.

MS: *Has teaching animation changed the way you work yourself?*

RL: On a good day I find my students' working processes incredibly exciting and inspiring. When you're teaching, there's always this terrible period when the students are trying to give birth to some kind of idea that's do-able and that's incredibly complicated and painful. But then, as a tutor there's this wonderful moment when they start actually making the work, and you come into school and there are lots of new bits of film to look at – that's wonderful and stuff is always unexpected.

It can be difficult to do your own work when you're teaching full-time though, because you use up that part of yourself. The job I'm doing at Harvard University this year is perfect, because I'm only teaching 10 hours a week in the expectation that I'll spend the rest of the time making my own work. It's fantastic and it's the first time that I've worked with such freedom since I left college. The problem with any kind of funding is that you have to describe what you're going to do to get the money and of course, it has to be like that. But what I'm doing at the moment is so much more exploratory because there's no one to say, 'Hang on, you said you were going to do this' – it can evolve.

MS: *Could you talk a bit about your idea of 'animation elsewhere'?*

RL: It's clear that the days when there was a lot of money available to make animation are now over, you cannot rely on getting funding to make your films for television – it's not going to happen if you're doing something halfway innovative or risky. So I think we have to look at other ways of making and showing films, and be very open about that. That's what 'animation elsewhere' is about, looking at other possibilities.

A big opportunity, which has really developed a lot, is animation in galleries. I've just been to the Museum of Modern Art in New York and the William Kentridge show there was fantastic – he's got a big room to himself, it's really well displayed and there's no question about what an animator's doing in an art gallery, it absolutely fits there. I think there's huge potential for that to develop. There's no reason why my work or many other animators' work shouldn't be displayed in art galleries to that slightly different audience.

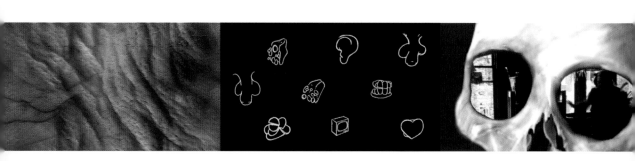

There are all sorts of different places in everyday life now where you can find moving images – mobile phones, screens on buses – and there are lots of ways our work could infiltrate into people's consciousness. Obviously there are compromises to be made, but in a way, showing your work on television isn't ideal either – I don't know what the other animate! animators think, but I always feel really peculiar and uncomfortable having the adverts on before and after my film, it's such a different world. So to show my work on a London bus would not necessarily be any more inappropriate than that. Music videos are obviously an area where art animation can happen too, and I just think we have to be alert to new ways of working.

The other thing we have to do is to be less feeble about making our own films without funding. I think if we're filmmakers, you shouldn't be able to stop us making films! We should be just doing it and a lot of my generation, and I've felt this myself, feel absolutely paralysed until someone not only gives you the money but gives you the official imprimatur, the stamp of approval to say that this is a film that's worth making. Really we should be able to do that for each other. I've been in a couple of groups where filmmakers are criting each other's work and encouraging each other, helping to develop each other's ideas, and I think that's the way forward.

animate! is now one of the very few ways of making your own work that's not commissioned in that very stultifying way. It's been very good for me, but I do think there's a problem when that's the only funding that's out there. I think it's important for animators to take risks and animate!'s failures are as important, in a way, as its successes. There has to be that space for people to try things out and see that they don't work too.

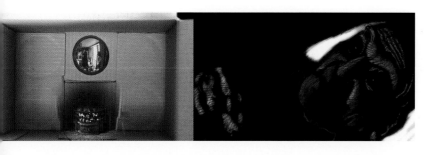

Tim Macmillan

Tim Macmillan studied Fine Art at Bath Academy and Experimental Media at Slade School of Art. During his studies he began to develop his signature time-slice technique; through the use of multiple aperture cameras, he created moving images in which his subjects seemed to be frozen in space. After working as a freelance photographer and studying Kyudo (Japanese archery) in Tokyo for several years, he returned to the UK and began to make films using time-slice. His installation piece Dead Horse (1998), portraying a horse at the moment of its death, brought him wide acclaim, and through his company Time-Slice Films he has continued to make work for television, advertising and feature films.

His first animate! film Ferment (1999) was a journey through his home town of Bath, observing its inhabitants in a frozen moment of everyday life. Animal Tragic (2003), his second commission, recreated three reported incidents of unfortunate interactions between animals and people.

MS: *Your work is very rooted in the photographic, which isn't perhaps the first thing people would associate with animation.*

TM: I was originally a painter and I went to Bath Academy to study painting. I was doing lifesize portraits in oils, stuff like that, very traditional. But I had a growing interest in Cubism, and ways of describing space and volume. In a Cubist painting or sculpture, you can incorporate various views – frontal views, plan views – all within the same image.

One day I just gatecrashed this workshop that one of the graphics tutors was doing and it was about making silver salt photographic emulsion, to Fox Talbot's original recipe. That rang all the bells with me – it appealed to me as a painter because I was making the paper by hand and painting on the emulsion and yet it was photographic, it reacted with light. So that got me interested in using the photographic process, but I didn't start making photographs, I initially just made photograms.

There were lots of experiments like that and it then progressed to making little cameras which I could put the negative in – very rudimentary, boxy pinhole cameras. I'd experimented with doing collage work, doing the Cubist thing, but it wasn't very successful. There seemed to be this fight between the concept and the way it was executed – collage just didn't really have a three-dimensional quality to it. So I sat down again and wondered, where do I go from here? And I thought, 'Why don't I take a strip of film and turn each frame into a pinhole camera? Then I can stick it in a projector and make a movie, instead of flipbooks and so on.' That seemed to me, conceptually, to work – there was nothing standing in the way of the concept, as with collage, it was much purer. You would go straight from points in space to the moving image.

So I built a camera using 16mm film and 16mm sound tape which had sprocket holes in it, so you could register it, and drilled pinholes in the sound tape. That produced an image – it was a bit blurry and fuzzy, because it was a pinhole down to a 16mm size negative. But it did prove the concept, that I could get a tracking shot, and not only did we have this journey through space, we suddenly had a journey through space without time as well.

Up to that point, I'd only considered the spatial aspects of the shot, I hadn't really considered time. But of course, the minute you animate something, you're concerned with time.

MS: *And did you think of it as animation, at this point, or were you thinking more in terms of sculpture, for example?*

TM: Neither – I had no point of reference in either of those fields, my only point of reference was painting. I didn't even own a regular camera then, I didn't take photographs. I'd had no formal training at all with photography, film or animation, so I was really following a conceptual idea and just using my intuition about how this was going to work – how do I translate this idea into an image? All the analysis about what this effect, the time-slice, means and how it fitted into film history, came much later. At that point, I was just following my nose.

Then I built a 35mm-based camera, which made much better images and I would send the film to the lab which would make a 16mm print which I could project. Those films were very successful. I was still making square cameras – it's easy to make a straight line of cameras, but very difficult to make a curve, because it needs very carefully engineered concentric planes. So I made a square camera, with four straight bits bolted together, so when you watched the film you'd go on a kind of rollercoaster ride, 360° around the subject. And that was my degree show piece at Bath.

Immediately after Bath I went to the Slade to do a postgraduate course where I built the first circular camera, because that's where it was heading really. I was still following the concept of recording space in a single moment of time and it seemed that a circle was going to be the ideal motif or camera move to express that. In a sense it becomes a continuous loop within that continuous moment – your eye isn't distracted by a sudden movement of the lens, going from looking one way to another way, it becomes a very coherent image. So I built the first circular camera and made films with that – things like a splash of water, jumping and other similar things.

For my degree show at the Slade, I decided to half-submerge the camera into a swimming pool and have somebody dive in. I got some shots, but the camera leaked and it was a step beyond my technical expertise at the time. But I was starting to think about the kind of subject matter which might work with this idea.

I also went colour as well. The early films were all black and white, I could develop them myself with a bucket, so that was fairly easy. At the Slade I started using colour film, which again, seeing as it was pinhole images, helps you to lock on to the image. There was no post-production at all – computers didn't exist for me at that point!

MS: *Who were you influences around that time?*

TM: I really wasn't looking outward at all, I was in my own little world. I was aware of Muybridge, and I was aware of Marey. I wasn't aware at that time that Muybridge had done simultaneous stuff as well, I just knew that he'd kicked off moving image by taking those sequential images of the galloping horse. Marey had done sequential images of locomotion, motion analysis. And the early pictures I was taking – things like people jumping or throwing a bucket of water – were more a reference to Muybridge – they were quite banal events, or surreal events. Muybridge would have a woman spanking a baby or something like that, and I was quite interested in the surreal nature of it.

There's always this struggle between Cubism and Surrealism in my work and although the concept was kind of Cubist in its nature, the actual outcome – the films – were very surreal, as they showed you a time and space which was impossible – like the portrait of Salvador Dali with everything flying in the air, the cat and the easel and the water.

After the Slade, I made a film through the London Film-makers' Co-op called *Spilt Milk* (1984). It was a breakfast scene and it was a bit of a complex thing which involved

some slides, some sound stuff and time-slice moments of me knocking over a bottle of milk on the breakfast table.

MS: *How was that received? Did you feel that it fitted into the work that was being made at the Co-op at the time?*

TM: Not at all, no. At that time, whenever I brought this work out into daylight people just went, 'What?' I remember once we had a joint screening with Royal College of Art people doing film and video, and the people from the Royal College were using old Umatic editing machines to do scratch videos of *Crossroads*, things like that. When my stuff came on, people just sat there totally blank.

When I showed stuff at University College, which the Slade is a part of, the artists would come along and say, 'It's amazing but it's a bit scientific', and the scientists would come along and say, 'That's amazing but it's very arty.' So I was on this road which was sci-art, which didn't exist at the time – the whole area's quite clearly defined now and there are a lot of artists who work in this space between science and art, but I was totally alone at that point. My only friend was David Curtis, then Artists' Film Officer at the Arts Council, who told me to keep going.

I went to Japan for several years and when I came back in 1990 I put in for a grant to the Arts Council. I got the grant, but I was going through some tough times then unfortunately – we'd come back right in the middle of a recession after the stock-market crash, and there were lots of photographers doing menial jobs. So the Arts Council grant got spent at Sainsbury's, I'm afraid to say. And every so often they'd call up and ask how it was going. And I'd say, 'Yes, it's coming along...' In the end, I think David Curtis got a bit frustrated, so he called up the television show *Tomorrow's World* and said, 'There's this guy with a camera making films, he's right up your street.' So *Tomorrow's World* called me up and said they wanted to feature me on the show a couple of weeks later.

I had to build a camera very quickly, so I turfed the family out of the house – they had to live upstairs, because the whole ground floor was taken up with a workshop for making the camera. We managed to get some film shot just in time for the *Tomorrow's World* broadcast, and that was the turning point. I made a film with a dog jumping, or rather being thrown, through a circular camera and it had quite a big impact. But even then, although it created a stir, nothing happened in terms of production companies or advertising agencies calling me up – but the people that did think it was extremely

interesting were the natural history people at the BBC in Bristol. They commissioned me to build some cameras and make some films, starting off with insects and gradually moving on to bigger things. That was in 1994, and from about 1995 I started to get more commercial work.

I think the moment of revelation was when I saw the *Tomorrow's World* broadcast and the public reaction to it and I thought, 'I know what this effect is and I know what I'm going to do with it now.' To do what I wanted to do with it, I had to go into commercials – in order to get the equipment, the technique and the money which I needed to do the artwork. So the ulterior motive was always to eventually do artwork, the first of which was *Dead Horse*.

Dead Horse and *Ferment* were two sides of the same coin. I knew what I wanted to make and one aspect of that with *Ferment* was this kind of motion picture animation, with tracking shots through scenes and a kind of narrative. The other aspect, with *Dead Horse*, was the single screen, single moment of time artwork, where it's more like a sculpture or a painting. So I had these two strands in my head after *Tomorrow's World*.

MS: *And at this point you were starting to think more in terms of the language of animation?*

TM: Yes. And I dug out my books on Eisenstein, the juxtaposition of images and so on. The moment I started working with the natural history people, there was a big coming to terms with dealing with motion pictures and television, anything that involves moving images edited together in a narrative. In the commercial work, I was having to marry this frozen moment with a narrative, which is always difficult – how do you freeze a moment, but keep the narrative moving? There was a long exploration of how to do that and as the years have gone by and people have become more used to the effect, editors become more creative and it becomes far more subtle and interesting.

MS: *But at the time,* Ferment *was one of the first films to use the technique.*

TM: Yes, I'd used it and other people had used the technique in pop videos beforehand, but as far as I'm aware that was the first short film that used it. So *Ferment* was quite an important moment – *Ferment* and *Dead Horse* were my first real works of art using the technique. I think I was only semi-conscious with my earlier films, I was going on instinct,

whereas with *Ferment* and *Dead Horse* I was going on what I really believed in.

MS: *With* Ferment, *how did you come to marry the technique to the subject matter of this tracking shot through the centre of Bath?*

TM: I was very into this idea of making a gigantic camera which would go right across the city, through buildings and everything, and if you could take a picture of one moment in time – what would that look like? Obviously, technically the idea of filming with an enormous camera and knocking holes through walls wasn't very good… But being a bit more film-savvy I thought, 'I can just shoot individual pieces and wipe them together to create this long tracking shot'.

So that's where the initial idea came from, and in order to create those scenes I went and hung out with these people. I drew a line on a map and sourced some places along the route – with some things, like the school, I had to go slightly off-route, but essentially the journey across the town could be in a straight line. I spent a day or so with each person and watched what they were doing and analysed it, so when I brought the camera along I could direct them – 'You wash the dishes, you're opening the fridge' and so on – based on what I'd seen them doing before. Because I knew from directing commercial stuff that if you tell somebody just to act normal they couldn't, you have to give them something to do. I tried to get a breadth of existence, even finding a couple that were happy to have some on-screen sex.

It was difficult though, because the facilities house where I'd been planning to post-produce the film closed their video department the week we started shooting. I was shooting stuff and not knowing how on earth I was going to post-produce it, and in the end I decided to buy the kit and do it in-house, so that kick-started Time-Slice Films.

MS: *What about* Animal Tragic (2004), *your second animate! film? Is it right that it was a kind of polemical response to some of the reactions you'd had to* Dead Horse?

TM: Yes, I'd become very fascinated by the animal rights scene in this country. There was a very strong reaction to *Dead Horse* – not from the people who saw it but from people who hadn't seen it, strangely enough. When it was shown at the Photographers' Gallery in London, a couple of newspapers sent reporters down to try to get some people coming out who would be throwing up and generally saying, 'This is horrendous', which

didn't happen – everyone came out saying that it was quite profound. What happened was that the local paper here in Bath caught wind of it and called some local artists saying, 'Some guy has taken a picture of a horse being shot as an artwork, what do you think of that?' And they all said it was outrageous and that got all the animal rights people steamed up. We went through a period of getting anonymous brown paper parcels through the door and tubes of cardboard with plasticine in them… That got me very interested in this friction between what animals actually are, which is what I'd been learning when I'd been doing the natural history filming, and the things that people think animals are, and the disparity between those two things.

So I thought, 'I'll take three stories from reading the local paper and I'll analyse the relationship between what animals are and what we think they are.' It was also that after *Ferment* I wanted to explore a more complex use of the technique with narrative, so with *Animal Tragic* there's a voiceover and intercutting scenes and it was a very difficult piece to make. If you work with children and animals, you really do need a producer! It was quite a lot to handle, trying to produce and direct at the same time, there were problems with the children and the animals and everything. It was quite an uphill struggle and it was such an emotional time, so when I finally finished it I just signed it off and then thought about other things. But this year I went out to Switzerland to see it in a couple of festivals and the response has been amazing, it really does strike a chord. So that's been very gratifying, to see that people really love it as an art piece and as a documentary piece, on all sorts of different levels.

MS: *How do you feel about animation generally?*

TM: Animation is such a broad field now. I find that my stuff is equally accepted as animation or documentary film, so I can slip into whatever clothes I like. It's quite an interesting situation to be in.

What is interesting is that animation is becoming its own thing. I was at the Norwich Animation Festival and somebody described it as like making poetry, because a poem is something that is kind of abstract – it defies being tied down to having a beginning, middle and end. And looking at animation work, there's a sense that the films are like visual poems – I really like that idea. It's a format in its own right, like a poem, and it's far more exclusive – lots of people read novels and far fewer people read poems, but I bet they remember them.

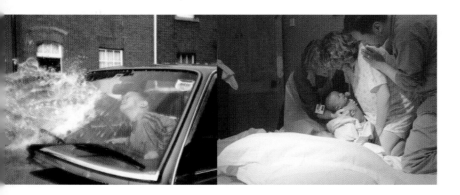

The idea about animation is that as the artist creates the image, they're able to distil a more potent feeling or effect – I really appreciate that, because I still have these painting sensibilities going round in my head and a lot of the single screen work I do obviously references painting. But I really do feel there is a need for that, and the audience responds to something that has been carefully crafted – in commercials and films and television you can lose that, because it's a group activity. With animation you have this single voice speaking to you and I like that.

Animal Tragic

**three stories
about people
and animals**

Animal Tragic Tim Macmillan (2003)/97

ROOM SERVICE

Room Service Sylvie Bringas (1991)/99

Build It and They Will Come: animate! and the Extended Imagination
Gareth Evans, with Dick Arnall

Come to the edge.
We might fall.
Come to the edge.
It's too high!
COME TO THE EDGE!
And they came,
And we pushed,
And they flew.
                    Christopher Logue

An abiding irony at the heart of what is, often optimistically, called British Cinema is the fact that, in its island incarnation, it is so often considered the realm of the formulaic, the hackneyed, the all-too tried and tested. Whereas those makers who have endured beyond their moment, and even those who (manage to) work today, and whose reputation reaches beyond their peer group and national borders, can all claim to occupy some experimental, oppositional or even transgressive position in relation to the dominant cinematic or televisual practices of their times.

So, whether it's Michael Powell or Derek Jarman, Humphrey Jennings or Lynne Ramsay, Alan Clarke or Sally Potter, the strain in British film and video that most honestly represents the seam of real achievement nationally is an enquiring, exploratory, innovative and ambitious one, refusing to rest on established models of expression, however successful.

In moving image terms, such an agenda has only been institutionally adopted, for obvious reasons, briefly and with varying degrees of reservation. Living memory examples of a counter to that are few: both the British Film Institute Production Board and the Arts Council of Great Britain (now Arts Council England) were, from the 1970s onwards, remarkable promoters of the maverick maker, interfacing in the early 80s with the only television channel fully to understand the value of such backing to the culture generally. It's dangerous to think too much in golden age terms, but there's no denying the territory-transforming impact Channel 4 made when it opened for business in 1982, from its pioneering structure as a publisher-broadcaster commissioning work across all formats in a way that had never previously been seen, to its undoubted early-years commitment to genuinely leftfield cultural and political fare. The fact that it combined a flexible, accessible production structure with a desire for ideas and imagination made it the natural habitat for the emergence of striking new visions and voices.

It was into such a hothouse in 1990 that animate! was born, providing a unique space within British structures for the creation and promotion of manipulated moving image work that is not primarily motivated by concerns of character and plot. Sixteen years on, it can claim, remarkably, to be the longest running broadcaster-linked project ever funded by Arts Council England and is maintained by the most consistent commitment ever made by Channel 4, or indeed any broadcaster world-wide, to the independent production of innovative and challenging film, video and digital work.

This longevity occurs not only because of the commitment and passions of key personnel in those organisations but also because, over the years, animate! has established itself as an arena in which established and emergent animators, artists and creative filmmakers can all experiment; [in] a space sanctioned for risk-taking and boundary crossing. Across dozens of films, animate! has developed an identity and attitude that is the opposite of monolithic, prescriptive or pre-emptive. This hydra-headed quality is fundamental to animate!'s successful position in the current moving image landscape, not least because it acknowledges the huge shifts in the nature of both animation practice and wider moving image infrastructures.

The fragmentation of creative industrial practices in the 1990s – the rise of garage geniuses, bedroom brains and music promo magicians conjuring images out of the unregulated air – was matched in importance only by the technological accelerations that made such endeavours possible. The almost definitive switch from film to the digital, the falling cost of home production hard- and software, and the exponential growth of the internet, all fed into a sector that was already experiencing the blurring of boundaries between art and commerce, between 'high' and 'low' cultural expression, between modes of distribution and exhibition, between the hands-on artist and the artist who hires hands.

Within such a creative and professional ferment, it is of course essential to remember that the prime formal objective of animate! has been to make single screen films for television transmission. Filmmakers always retain the copyright and ownership of their works (bar Channel 4's free licence to two UK transmissions), what happens afterwards – whether festival run or supporting short or gallery installation – is open.

So, animate! makers are the literal engines – creative and technical – of their prod-uctions. animate! is a midwife, it does not produce individual projects, it funds and supports them. However, there is perhaps a certain clarity in that original televisual remit that remains unchanged. The infinite treasure chest that is the digital toolbox can sometimes serve to paralyse choice: aesthetic decisions are potentially limitless. While answers to those questions remain the prerogative of the artist, the fixed frame of television also requires the artist's creative journey to be accompanied by a considera-tion of 'real world' technical parameters and legal underpinnings (initially to enable their work to be broadcast on Channel 4) but thereby ensuring that there will be no barriers to the film's fuller and longer life beyond this first outing. In short, what might work there – and television is, by some margin, the hardest moving image medium to win over – provides a necessary and rigorous frame within which to test and play.

Television also, importantly, puts experimental animation into the wider culture, even if only briefly, providing a genuine opportunity for the chance encounter that might change a viewer's preconception of what the moving image is for. That ripple of animation outwards is also found in animate!'s commissioning, given that it invites applications from anyone, whether they consider themselves an animator or not.

And finally, it allows makers to concentrate on what matters most: the creation of a personal vision that extends the possibilities of what the moving image can hold and deliver, while speaking about issues, emotions and ideas that concern us all.

In an essay(1) important to animate!, pioneering independent producer and animate! co-instigator Keith Griffiths voices core concerns, observing that now every Hollywood blockbuster passes, in its entirety, through a digital gateway between its filming and its release print. So what happens in front of the camera is merely pixel-grist for the digital 'mill'. He argues that the possibility to digitally manipulate every single frame of live action film returns the form to the realm of animation. Therefore, the computer's intervention in 'post-production' can now be liberated in pursuit of 'hallucinations of reality'.

As mainstream cinema moves deeper and deeper into digital intervention (whether visible or invisible) in its construction of synthetic space, characters and action, animators could be grasping the vast opportunities afforded to them by their instinctive understanding of the potent manipulation of the moving image. But those who still see animation simply as a frame-by-frame process, akin to an incrementally extending line of dominos butted together, or merely as special effects to be considered in 'post-production', will never be amongst the real creative visionaries and art directors devising this extended cinema.

Take this fully on board and animate! as a concept and a word contains the etymological seed of its own success. It brings to life; it inspires. How a culture sees, what it looks at or doesn't, what it allows into the frame, makes it or breaks it. animate! seeks to make a space for the extended moving image only because it believes in the extended imagination. By crafting worlds before us, it underscores its constant belief in the 'possible' being of more interest than the 'probable'. Build it and they will come.

Cowboys (1991) Phil Mulloy

The first completed animate! commission, Phil Mulloy's extraordinary 1991 re-visioning of the iconography of the Western genre, in some ways signposts the primary intentions, intellectually and contextually, of the project as a whole. All animation creates worlds that suspend conventional logic and expectations; in this way the form itself claims softly subversive credentials. But how quickly the most conventional of those approaches –

humorously atomised bodies, perverse gravities and impossible scale shifts – register a new conservatism, against which a kind of animated dirty realism or a truly inflected, visionary geography needs, must launch its own counter assault.

The genuine subversion and repositioning of familiar imagery in such a way as to challenge accepted values and assumptions, whether aesthetic or thematic, lies at the core of animate!'s agenda, but it is rarely expressed as cogently or with such melancholic wit as in Mulloy's sextet of satirical scenarios. Casting his scrawled models of masculinity into the heart of the contemporary crisis, he proceeds to illustrate, in a drawn visual language of extreme economy, herd motivations around consumerism, media manipulation and the society of the spectacle, the easy violence of the mob and its embedded contempt for otherness, along with its hypocrisy concerning desire and sexual expression, in three-minute episodes fuelled by a savage despair.

While the targets are broad and broadly attacked, the complexity of Mulloy's response, indeed, the humanising element in his 'cartooning', lies in the subtleties of detail. For each very effective moment where a shock of red (flames of erectile threat, the bared fangs of vulture squadrons) invades the black and white landscapes, there is a quieter intervention or signing off, around which much of the real intent might turn. Such as the final shot of *That's Nothin'* (1991), which holds on the gently closing eye of a sodomised horse, the victim of an accelerated sexual showdown, accompanied by the smallest of sighs, a breathing out that suggests everything from involuntary satisfaction to a final, existential rupture (this subtlety comes care of Mulloy's own moans, part of a precise soundscape that also includes the gleefully well-judged scoring of Alex Balanescu).

Run this alongside the sweeping scale of both scenes and psychologies in *The Conformist* (1970), perhaps the most concisely incursive and peerlessly bleak instalment, and the evidence is strong that politically inflected work of significant reach can work to great effect in the seemingly most constrained format. Fifteen years on, it might be hard to recall the shock felt in some quarters at both Mulloy's content and the rawness of his brush-and-ink marking; but *Cowboys* remains unsettling and provocative viewing: a project that it is effectively impossible to imagine the British broadcast media supporting now. In his first entirely animated work, Mulloy signalled his refusal to conform.

Soho Square (1992) Mario Cavalli

Also commissioned in the first year, but at the other spectrum end from Mulloy's radical horse hustlers, Mario Cavalli's animation-as-celebration of place and its seemingly easy-living population might at first appear all too thematically comfortable; a pastel picture of community encounters in a green shade that, if frozen, one might mistake for a Hallmark vision of human interaction.

However, the devil's always in the detail. Cavalli is a leading industry animator; he knows the heart of the media hub – this micro-park, this urgent green lung – as well as anyone and is far too able and savvy to the often melancholy state of things to deliver just the rose-hued. There is 'reality' aplenty in his rigorously rendered work, from bench-end drunkenness, through a wider dereliction, to the undermining urban isolations at the heart of a horde. All too often unmarked sadness occurs within what remains a space aspiring to the utopian (as all parks do, in conception if nothing else), and suggests that such a landscape, and here animation as well, might restore, redeem even, the fallen. The form not only dismembers, wrenches apart and fragments previously complacent dimensions – as so many cartoons do – it can celebrate, can seed hope.

But of course *Soho Square* is as much a dream space as it is an actually existing site, whatever its character. And it is made with an ahead-of-the-curve digital intervention, the provenance of which is perhaps completely lost on virgin viewers in this most pixilated of new centuries. Firstly, a live action video diary was shot on Hi8, which was then edited into a storyboard of shots that became, with choreographic aid, a series of restaged 'performances' by mime artists in a blue screen studio. However, where blue screen technology allows the superimposition of remote landscapes behind the participants, Cavalli sought further alterations, dressing the performers in colour-coded clothing that allowed him to digitally change the hues and densities of colour in the final image. In other words, according to a pre-conceived design, he sought to give 'paint' a human origin and movement.

Soho Square therefore seeks a fusion of the manipulated and the extant with an eye that could only belong to an animator (the same is viscerally true of *Dad's Dead* (2003), Chris Shepherd's multi award-winning chorale of collapse, an animation-driven montage with live action.) The key turns when a hose-wielding gardener hands a bottle out of frame.

But from which frame to where, which world to what offstage location? There is a threshold but it is a multiple co-existent one. This is not animation as illustration but, in a manner, animation as Blakean examination, looking closer and closer for the clue in the form and the formed, the heaven in a wild flower, the pastoral eternity in the rush hour.

Biogenesis (1993) William Latham

Where *Soho Square* deploys the digital, the better to re-vision the world as it might be, William Latham's coded 'digital garden' inhabits its technology entirely. It exists nowhere but in its ones and zeros, yet posits a world with its own inexorably unfolding logic and at the same time willing suspension of disbelief, that could label itself equally utopian. Originally to be called *The Creation*, Latham's vision was the product of a programming team working directly on an IBM mainframe computer (the last film indeed to be made in this way, closing a chapter started by the Corporation's sponsoring of the first computer animation by the Whitney Brothers). It posits a simulacrum of evolution, a self-evolving structure of fractal scale shifts that nods to the iconography of *Alien* (1979) as much as to DNA spirals or the oily deliria of old-school light shows.

In this way it has antecedents (and in animate! terms, turns the soil years in advance for works like Andrew Kötting's *Kingdom Protista* (2000)) but also refuses any ancestry, any evidence of lineage towards its own being. An artificial life form mutating ceaselessly in the vacuum-sealed hothouse of silicon space, it is the perfect creature for our times. It promises infinite visual possibility (Jem Finer's thousand year long non-repeating music piece *Longplayer* might be its iPod choice) but in real terms is locked into the restrictive grid of its own soft- and harder-ware options. A crucial experiment, the significant question it raises about the relationship between imagination (and its limits), technology and the animated application of those tools, is one it cannot alone answer, except by providing one benchmark of the relative potentials.

It is a work that marks a liminal moment in both animate!'s development but also in a wider understanding of how self-sustaining systems can seed and thrive within the realm of the digital. In Latham's own words, '*Biogenesis* shows the evolution of artificial life forms in a synthetic universe where "survival of the fittest" is replaced by "survival of the most aesthetic".'

The description 'most aesthetic' might be contestable but what is not up for debate is that *Biogenesis* does deliver a kind of binary epiphany, if one appreciates, or rather, constantly reminds oneself that this 'cellular evolution', this 'coral' of replication is almost the Adam, the primal 'digital soup' creature hauling itself onto the beach of the early computer screen, destined to beget by inference and association so much of the visual realm within which we now live. Latham's sense of himself as a gardener, and of the work as 'a subtle parody of man's relationship with the natural world through modern technology' is viable, but seen from here, he is perhaps closer to a biotechnologist of the cyber, a nano-manipulator of our visual futures.

Devising algorithms to make evolutionary selections according to programmed notions of 'beauty', he married the very core of the emergent paradigm with the oldest impulse of humankind, operating in this primary way within a hardware and a corporate hierarchy that lived, for the vast majority of its day, far from such intentions. For this alone, *Biogenesis* remains one of animate!'s most distinctive commissions.

What She Wants (1994) Ruth Lingford

Latham's fecund flotsam and jetsam was the writhing offspring of the mainframe, but real life and its capture requires something a little closer to the street. When that life has the fleshly intensity of Ruth Lingford's equally metamorphosing journey through a sexualised cityscape, then it seems counter intuitively surprising to think it might be the provocative lovechild of a relationship between artist and machine. Yet, remarkably, *What She Wants* was created on a home Amiga system, a digital video engine designed for gaming, with numerous sequences of just a few seconds, each stored on 40 floppy discs (it had no hard drive).

The machinery is now obsolete, but the content is far from redundant. Just as Lingford delivered, simply in the making, a potent pitch for gender and its representation within the almost inherently masculine ambience of the emergent technology, so the film itself infuses a subject arena again more often dominated by the male with a complex feminism. But hers is no placard-proud sloganeering. This is an anatomy of wanting, not action points. As her protagonist navigates the charged environments of the metropolis, the tension for Lingford is between control and abandon (providing a useful metaphor

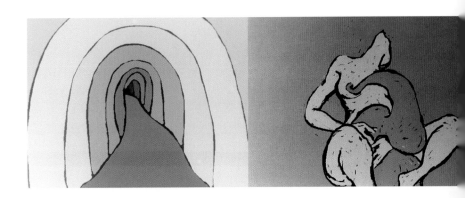

for the challenges of working within animation itself), between submission and engagement. It is a constantly shifting argument that takes place internally but is here visualised as a desire path, a tactile map, felt in the body but given to the map, through yearning towards learning.

In the spirit of Susan Pitt's similarly path-breaking *Asparagus* (1978), one consumes and is consumed, makes a new picture of oneself while caught in (art) historical image claims, from Goya to fairy tales via the motif of the mother as nurturer and victim. A truly ambiguous exploration of secret, half-voiced imperatives, it can in no way be reduced to an easy tract against commodification and the hostile gaze of the besuited other. This interweaving of attitudes is sharpest in the image of the purse, a structurally feminine object that nevertheless enables a masculine purchase power, and in the startling final image of a crone-faced moth-woman, flying free of the city and its lusting compromises, its endless negotiations, but at what cost? The implication is that the thrash and wrestle of the daily both fetters and fuels those living impulses.

Animation here reveals itself as the form perhaps most able to hold visual incarnations of longing, simply because, when it comes to desire, the slippage between realities and the attendant changes in emotional register, are so fluid that other media have trouble maintaining the required subtlety and grace of passage.

Feeling My Way (1997) Jonathan Hodgson

The echoes, the amplifications, the synchronicities and distinctions multiply as the animate! assembly swells. Ruth Lingford stepped out through the eroticised urban. Mario Cavalli planted the processed alongside his preening, prowling, playful parklife. Jonathan Hodgson also took a personal path through the sign-surplused city, also packed an Amiga, but his live action walk to work in Soho, his video diary of the day's noise in- and outside the head, becomes a means to a mash-up end, a way to archive the mental graffiti, the Joycean bubble and froth as it spills into the street and vice versa, the world's unkempt business washing in through eyes and ears, through pores.

The title indicates the strata, of course: from the physicality of his process, entering an animated unknown, to the perennial unpredictability of the pedestrian incursion into the

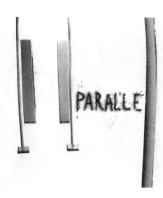

wider whole. The commute, then the day's labour; so when is his film's making really to be done? At night of course. When else does one make a mortality movie; when else does one find and confirm the skeleton inside the suit, the solitary in the surge, except in the dark hours? He acquired an early HP industrial inkjet printer, took his footage – the graphic interventions into already low-end video – set the printer to batch output through the night and produced 100 frames by morning. The Amiga software was a long way from stable. Some dawns there were just a couple of sheets in the tray. The distressed became more so.

The newly imagined city, the city as read, is already scuzzed (the print technology confirms this – poor video print outs – but that was the point, the sensation), yet it is still as much mythic as it is mundane. Detritus and excess yield the insights of ages and the timelessly trivial, or sometime personally timeless. The click of a stick along museum railings brings Proustian recall of school walk ruler rattles, of a tactile encounter with the city that breaks us momentarily clear of all the head work, all the business done and processed behind the eyes.

Again, as with desire, animation of this hue thrives on overload, on the mixed message, the hybrid home from home of the multifarious real. It pretends to classify, but because its system is based on the most idiosyncratic of ordering agencies, an individual human imagination, it cannot help but install systemic flaws into the heart of its arrangement. The subjective is everywhere in its would-be archive of experience: selective, distracted, tired, troubled. It is in the glitches and gaps made by the human that the life of the project breathes: the proverbial (experiential and aesthetic) flagstone weed that will topple the monoliths of tired, dead cultures.

Withdrawal (1997) George Barber

Where Hodgson's walk took him from the relatively reduced signage of the domestic into the staccato 'noise' of the street, renowned artist video-maker and found footage 'scratch' pioneer George Barber's fable of mounting absences flags up an ascetic impulse that perhaps lies at the heart of the digital excess; a whispering counterpoint, a kind of white space within the infinite palette of technical and creative possibilities that pixel manipulation now affords.

Among Barber's most affecting and skilful weaves of the material with the metaphysical, this telling mortality haiku accumulates digital erasures, formally simple but thematically 'animating'. He offers a seeming pastoral idyll, a green meadow stretching to trees and mountains beyond, all under the perfect blue of sky, its drifting clouds offering no threat of rain. In a series of short scenes, a relaxed and seemingly extended family group walk happily towards and past the camera. Each time they do so however, their number reduces, along with certain features of the landscape.

Finally we are left with a single boy, walking on just the earth itself, devoid of flora and foliage. Accompanying the entire process have been fragments of dialogue on life and the passing of things from voices of all ages. As the boy leaves the frame for the last time, the camera pans slowly up from the now empty planet to the constellations far above. The measuring of human time and its stories against this vastness is conveyed precisely and poignantly.

The creative tension here, the dynamic that underpins all of Barber's work, is between the unframed beneficence and fecundity of genuine human conduct, evidenced in the warm chatter of *Withdrawal*, and a certain arrival at a certain kind of threshold, with its gleaming promise of brief rest from the workings of the world and all its images. In its visible construction, its less than hyper-real assembly (which gifts much of the poignancy to the wide themes explored) and its self-declared imperative to retreat from the overspill of images, *Withdrawal* stands as a quietly significant way marker in the animate! landscape, almost an anti-animation, a reminder both of what else the medium does and that less can most definitely yield more.

Ferment (1999) Tim Macmillan

But, for an artist, withdrawal is not a sustainable career option. The teeming urban, siren-like, calls them back. The pleasures of the flâneur, the movement through spaces and lives: these are blood pumps to the animator. What else is richer than a walk through the world as it is and could be? The dynamic intangibles of the immediate daily. Sensory exploration then, for purposes of singular retrieval, but few find themselves with the equipment Tim Macmillan can boast. It's not often someone invents a technology that grants perception the palpable jolt of an encounter with the previously unseen, in the way that time-slice offers.

When he first called it into the world in 1980 (as what he came to discover was only the most recent in a long historical line of similarly remarkable ocular re-visioning engines), Macmillan believed he was exploring space, testing perceptual limits around the dimensions of topography. It was only later that he understood fully he was investigating the visual identity of time, of the beat that one's heart skips when the frame rests. His gallery piece *Dead Horse* (1998) introduced this timeline to the public. It was a walk along the conceptual high wire where the still and moving image become believably one. When timeline then grows into narrative, *The Matrix* of possibilities is vast. So a progress through Bath, from colonnade to council block, Georgian square to bathtub romp, becomes a frozen theatre of the human story in all its infinite recurrence.

But it's a mark, if any were needed, of the acceleration of the technological moment, as well as an undeniable tribute to the reorienting abilities of the eye–brain relationship, that we all too soon take the new looking as a given, as a regular component of the kit-box. Animation is necessary more than anything else because it extends the parameters of the eye, of what the eye, mind and heart must do fully to experience.

Love is All (1999) Oliver Harrison

Far in its machinery from time-slice's hi-end toolkit, *Love is All* might not initially call attention to its making and message with the showcase flair of Macmillan's work, but that does not mean the labour expended on this affectionate Deanna Durbin-driven ode to cinema history is any the less, nor is the distinctive vision diminished. As befits its aesthetic, this really is one of those animate! titles that, despite the project's undeniably televisual originating impulse, should be seen and enjoyed in a theatrical surround, where its oceanic currents of celluloid grain can draw one in and in.

Appropriately, one of the few recent animate! commissions actually made on film, *Love is All* reveals, as its title suggests, a complete and painstaking commitment on the filmmaker's part. The sometime pain of being that the song's lyrics convey, the exquisite obsession that love asks of its activists, is of course mirrored in Harrison's – and by association, all serious animators' – long-end investment in both craft and creation. Designing an optical printer specifically for this project, he made sometimes more than

20 passes through its gate to create the multi-layered, animated image vignettes that so enhance the finished artefact.

The result is a sensory dreamscape that seeks to convey the essence of affection, for a particular beloved, but also for a language, a vision of the world and its ways. Gentle sister to the warped historo-visions of Winnipeg maverick Guy Maddin, *Love is All* provides an ongoing and reverential bridge back towards the medium's origins, to the founding passions that fuelled both filmic form and content, while maintaining a knowing place inside current practice, where the consumables of a supposedly ephemeral and shallow popular culture find enduring resonance through repositioning and benign appropriation.

Rotting Artist (2002) Ann Course and Paul Clark

Perhaps surprisingly, the optimistic assertion that 'love is all' could well serve as the unspoken coda to Ann Course and Paul Clark's coruscating and inventive exploration of the transformative potency of art. Created as a Communard-style barricade against the various sensations – crushing oppression, whether personal or collective, rigid isolation and the existential level of despair in the species' capacity to violence in whatever form – *Rotting Artist* is one of animate!'s most profound and repeatedly rewarding works, evidence that the project can accommodate the broadest range of visual languages and subversive intentions (indeed, this feels like the kind of film that animate! was spiritually established to serve).

From the outset, *Rotting Artist* sets itself defiantly against its canonised soundtrack (the excessively familiar gallop of Beethoven's Ninth), while slyly stealing the tempo as pacing of the image trawl. Created from a series of Ann Course's occasionally shocking black-mark drawings of sometimes recognisable objects, structures, shapes and organo-aspirant forms (with the sequencing made associatively and spontaneously live on the rostrum camera and driven by playback of the music), the work rides in on the back of Ludwig's stallion with a brazen confidence that it too has as much claim to greatness as the symphony. And the trick is, it does. Conflict, authoritarianism and submission, the complex nature of sexuality, mortality itself; all are explored, briefly caught in a clash of images and actions and then given to the wind as the free flowing rush of moments

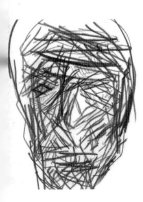
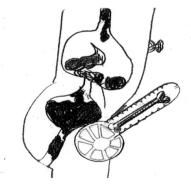

moves inexorably on, powered by the Ninth, a kind of wannabee humvee fuel.

Line and rhythm is the key here, sometimes of the world's terrain, at others, of the imagination's obscure terrain. But however seemingly abstracted some of the 'players' and their pursuits, the rigorous intentions, aesthetic and thematic, are never lost. Nodding to the Old Masters in several of its compositions, for strength of framing and again for legacy-linking purposes, it gazes relentlessly on attendant horrors. However, in its final image – of a solitary profiled eye – melancholy with the Goyaesque horrors it has witnessed but still quietly oppositional and open, the film seems to offer an affirming contrast (across all the lost decades) to the sliced vision of *Un Chien Andalou* (1929), to the sight that is irrevocably abused.

A kind of non-narrative return to the rough horse wranglers of Phil Mulloy's *Cowboys*, *Rotting Artist* shakes and stirs like all great art should, prompting us to consider the world and its often wicked ways afresh, to find form in the formless, empathy in the seemingly emptiest gesture and hope in the dark and even dirtied corners of the soul. We are all rotting artists, it declares, in mordantly witty pastiche of Joseph Beuys, and most of the time we remember neither the fact of our imminent dispersal, nor our creative potential: dwelling too long in the mediocre imperatives of the rat run and forgetting the maggot that yearns for our flesh from its endless loam. Few films offer a more startlingly concise wake up call.

Perpetual Motion in the Land of Milk and Honey (2004) AL + AL

Rotting Artist is an undeniably personal expression of emotional and psychological concerns. At first view, AL + AL's epic digital smorgasbord seems to be cut from a very different kind of cloth. But the world and references at play in this important, stakes-raising commission are equally intimate to this decidedly singular duo of makers, even if the surface is shined to a gloss and the visual references are to Britney Spears rather than to Hieronymus Bosch. AL + AL, however, have taken things a step further than many. In their east London live/work studio ('we're living in a special effects machine'), they permanently inhabit a blue screen environment, immersing themselves in the virtual space so totally they have almost become the Gilbert and George of this other 'reality'. And it's not with especially subversive intent that they have crossed the portal, although it's true that their image making lies mega pixels from the banalities of the mainstream.

Rather, AL + AL have welcomed the digital as a space in which personal and familial autobiography can be most creatively realised.

Cut to the humane kernel of *Perpetual Motion...* and what you find is an endearing homage to a grandfather, who aspired and worked from his garden shed to create a ceaseless energy source to liberate the masses from toil and want. A specifically English eccentric, he operates now at the heart of a vast machinery, a Metropolis of hugely imaginative reach, in which a cast of thousands strive to realise his utopian vision. This core conceit fuels a dazzlingly realised architecture built on a myriad of iconography probably only fully decipherable to AL + AL themselves. But what distinguishes it from a quasi-surreal pot-pourri is that the internal logic of their enterprise, and the beating heart of its homage to a beloved family member, is quickly apparent.

Perhaps, in this productive liaison of form and content, *Perpetual Motion...* serves as a significant pointer to the future direction moving image practice might take. animate! has always sought to extend the possibilities of the moving image, and with it the imagination of both makers and audiences, without losing sight of the fact that work is nothing if it is not finally *about* something. In their complete embrace of the digital, AL + AL represent the present and currently conceivable future. In their redirection of pop cultural pointers they are of this time and place, just as they are in their drawing on familial narratives for their firing material. But they understand implicitly that the ancient concerns, the preoccupations of long since rotten artists, with their desires and delusions, weaknesses and hopes, must underpin the infinite choice of possible surfaces and schema. Far from dwelling as ghosts in the machine, AL + AL, along with all those artists who share their values, have chosen to reclaim the pixilated palette from the market-meisters for pictures of the gone world and of all the myriad worlds yet to be born.

So, as with the project's strongest titles and with the form in general, the pleasures of the 'unreal' might be what first hook us, but it's the telling enquiries into the all-too-human real that keep us watching, keep us dreaming, keep us animate!

Endnotes

1 From www.animateonline.org/editorial/2001/04/the-manipulated-image

114/*Jukebox* (storyboard) Run Wrake (1994)

HALF LIVES
SARAH BEAUVOISIN
MARK BISHOP
NICK CURREY
SAMUEL DORE
FIONA STANILAND

Half Life Matt Hulse (2004)/119

Occupation: Animation and the Visual Arts
Ian White

In 1936 the German artist-filmmaker-animator Oskar Fischinger was denounced as degenerate by the Nazi government. With an already established aesthetic that was anchored in the often astonishing, resonant relationship between (largely abstract) images and sound, he left the animation studio he had established and emigrated to Los Angeles. He began work in the factory system of the Hollywood studios – Paramount, MGM – and in 1938 for Walt Disney on *Fantasia* (1940). At Disney he was respected as an artist (weekly screenings of his films were held for the staff's appreciation), belittled as an employee (earning $60 a week as a 'motion picture cartoon effects animator') and resented – if not hounded – as a co-worker who was overly celebrated. On 1 September 1939 Germany invaded Poland. That same day a swastika was pinned to Fischinger's door and he immediately sought the termination of his contract that was finally granted on 31 October.

How such an apparently bizarre collapse of political understanding intersects with the industrialised workplace is not entirely the subject of this essay. Nor is how art and the artist might be defined in the context of this political chaos – against, through or within a political system to which they are otherwise marginal. Rather, the essay presents a proposition about animation, and attempts to open up a definition of animation to incorporate visual art that would not ordinarily be considered as such.

In the most general of senses animation might be considered as the transformation of static, two-dimensional images or objects into motion, the illusion of life or abstract rhythm, the exploitation of the possibilities that such a process affords – fantasy, making the impossible imaginable, defying laws of nature and physical boundaries. The proposition I would like to make is supported by the application of this general definition to the work of the artists Paul McCarthy, VALIE EXPORT and Catherine Sullivan. In their different practices are examples of animation rendered physically (in the body) and conceptually (as part of the works' formal strategies) that are developed through the artists' common interest in the metaphor and the various actualities of occupation. In turn, the work of these artists opens the discussion to a political, social and aesthetic axis upon which animation might operate and through this, to how animation might – perhaps surprisingly – define a/our condition.

In 2005 the American artist Paul McCarthy and his son Damon jointly authored an epic installation work, *Caribbean Pirates*, based on the theme park ride Pirates of the Caribbean at Disneyland in Anaheim, California. Four years in the making, the work was exhibited at the Haus der Kunst, Munich and later in a slightly reordered exhibition at Whitechapel Gallery, London (where I saw it) as the major component of a show that at both venues was called *LaLa Land Parody Paradise*. *Caribbean Pirates* consisted of large-scale sculpture, modified found objects and video projection. There were three boats: an adapted houseboat (*Houseboat*) with one side removed, a television set on a worktop playing a film noir; a massive, steel mock-up of a slightly scaled down, rusting frigate (*Frigate*); and a mounted, moving ship constructed from a geometrical metal frame lined with wood (*Underwater World*), a fairground ride that the viewer could not enter. *Houseboat* and *Frigate*, along with an odd wooden platform and walkway (*Cakebox*), displayed signs of heavy usage – destruction, even. Smeared with Hershey's chocolate syrup, the empty cans of which littered these macabre structures, other dried fluids, half-destroyed furniture, the occasional, clearly fake, 'amputated' limb, the dormant machines, buckets and spray guns used to wreak this havoc and other signs of former habitation, the whole felt no less terrible because of its simulated blood and film set lighting rig. The scene was a typical yet still unholy reformulation of the all-American products that McCarthy has used in his work since the mid-1970s when ketchup and mayonnaise replaced his own bodily fluids.

In London the installation was housed in a warehouse, a short walk from the gallery proper where related drawings and objects were displayed. Not much other than the minimum required for safety reasons had been done to alter the original condition of this run down, functional space. Derelict offices surrounding the main floor housed video projections of ersatz schmaltz (tropical islands floating in clear blue seas turning upside down and rocking from side to side, a group of day-glo, over-eager carol singers playing forwards and – Satanically – backwards) were asymmetrically thrown onto rough walls, across corners, over cutaways. Two specially constructed projection areas above and alongside the boats, were made of gallery standard white boards. One showed three images side-by-side, roughly lined up, sloppily overlapping. The other, three white-boarded walls of an adjoining room, the fourth side of which opened on to the main floor, showed four off-centre, angled and overlapping images, arranged across its corners, slipping onto the corrugated iron ceiling, *Pirate Party*. Such an ordered chaos of successive, if different, images looked like an arrangement borrowed from one of Eadweard Muybridge's 19th century chronophotographs showing the passage of a body in motion over time. The coherent image appeared literally broken across a number of projection planes. The successive frames of animation.

What was being broken down by this manic exhibition of successive frames, of scenes that otherwise had a chronological relationship to each other being seen simultaneously, was the elaborate performance conducted on the pirate ship sets by Paul McCarthy in his role as First Mate, captured on video by Damon McCarthy. First Mate, a band of pirates and their acolytes (men and women, some in outsized cartoon-inspired grotesque fake heads) invade, rape, pillage and occupy an island. The literal destruction they effect is mirrored and codified by their morally disintegrated, infectious behaviour, the physical abuse they inflict on the inhabitants, their gratuitous, rampant (and perverted) sexual appetites, gross exhibitionism and exploration/exploitation of their own bodies and the bodies of others, literally or by association. The exhibition catalogue reflects the excess. It is large, with a slightly padded cover. Page after opulent page shows details and images of seemingly crazed, pirate-themed drawings (ships and pirates' noses metamorphosing into penises, pornography and advertising), installation shots and video stills. In it, John Welchman, reports from the set and lends a linear perspective to what occurred:

> We are in a village as it is attacked and occupied by the marauding pirates… The boy is verbally abused, repeatedly asked about the whereabouts of treasure, then tied up and subjected to a horrendous routine of torture and dismemberment. First a slice is taken out of his bulbous (fake) nose, then his (false) right ear is slit, and finally, the First Mate takes an axe to his fake but elaborately simulated left leg, smashing and hacking until he gets right through the 'bones'. The villager howls and wails, his stump spews blood… the pirates dance and cavort in voyeuristic ecstasy. Looking on to this scene are three village sisters wearing wench costumes… They moan, writher, chant, and grimace, like a cross between harpies, sirens, and a dissolute rendition of the three graces… their hollers and screams are accompanied by an increasingly gymnastic display of affected passion.(1)

What Welchman describes as linear, in the multiple projection of the exhibition, is itself dismembered. What he describes as present, in the exhibition, has actually passed. Damon McCarthy's wild video camera mimics the general state of disorientation, leering towards its subjects, turning them upside down, casually, chaotically, relentlessly. The soundtracks from each projected image are mixed into a single source that can be heard throughout the whole installation, signalling and conditioning responses. Even from its beginning, with what is to come being seen even alongside the planning of the pirates' assault, there are screams, whelps and human-animal wailing. While Paul McCarthy may have developed a structure for this improvised marauding and while First Mate may well have had a plan of attack, not only does the recorded action appear as destruction performed to its own spiralling volition, but its subsequent exhibition refuses the viewer the security of narrative. In this continuous, hideous charade there are no epiphanies, no Hollywood endings.

At the same time as we come to realise that everything in this used up film set installation relates to something having happened, we become aware that it is a particular definition of our own witnessing that becomes the overriding content of the work. While the discarded props, the smell of rotting, smeared chocolate sauce, broken furniture, the vessels that display these things relate, like proof, to the world of the projected images. The two things together, the object and the image, establish truth-values for each other (this is where they sat, this is what used, here is the limb) that implicate the viewer as a necessary function of their construction. Being trapped between them effects the erosion of critical distance in favour of inane entertainment, the troubling aspect of which becomes the comparative ease with which we witness these things, the familiarity with what is expected of us and a curiously familiar pattern of indulgent reception.

The description of Pirates of the Caribbean on the Disneyland Resort website entices us to, 'Set sail from an 1860's Louisiana Bayou as a rag-tag band of marauding pirates has overtaken a Caribbean village, ransacking and setting ablaze everything in sight – including yer boat if yer not careful, matey!' In a bullet point we are encouraged to, 'Revel in the comic fun of swashbuckling shenanigans.'(2) *Caribbean Pirates* mimics and assimilates the ride's component parts, but is most truly horrifying in the content it makes of these promises. It is a strategy we could understand as extending to Paul

Caribbean Pirates Paul McCarthy and Damon McCarthy (2001-2005)
Off site installation at Coppermill House during *Lala Land Parody Paradise* at the Whitechapel Gallery, (October 2005-February 2006)
Photo: Ben Johnson. Courtesy the artist/Whitechapel Gallery, London/123

McCarthy's practice in general. His studio adopts the form of the sprawling system of the Hollywood production machine in which Oskar Fischinger found himself,(3) and in the context of this work develops a grand metaphor of (artistic) production and (public) consumption. Welchman describes artistic practice, like the fake bodies of our protagonists, taken to the extremity of its own – and our – complicity:

> In *Caribbean Pirates* the studio [McCarthy's] becomes an enormous lair swarming with actors and extras, assistants and special effects people, film crews, technicians, and hangers-on. At some moments the professional apparatus is deployed as it would be in a Hollywood film set; at others the on- and off-camera worlds merge without jurisdiction, just as the sets and props shift from backdrops and objects to the different valences of sculpture and installation.(4)

Caribbean Pirates not only plays out occupation as torture-by-comic-strip, it also occupies the forms of entertainment which are its content. This is the occupation of a form in order to animate it and at the heart of this animation, in the installed work itself, the projected videos, we are not transported as in the theme park ride, but physically move ourselves. *We* occupy, *we* animate this animation in a double deathblow to the fantasy of escape that we would otherwise be sold.

The McCarthy–Disney equation then inevitably extends to government and a wider set of politics and contemporary international relations. Welchman cites Africa, Iraq, Haiti. *Caribbean Pirates* lends profundity to an anecdotal swipe at President George W. Bush that Dave Hickey takes in his *Vanity Fair* article on Florida's Walt Disney World. Hickey ventures into the animatronic Hall of Presidents:

> A music video about the constitution opened the show. Its broad generational appeal was followed by a softly lit tête-à-tête with a coterie of American presidents… The avatar of our current president stepped up to the plate and delivered a short homily that, I swear, the man might have written himself… Of all the animatronic presidents, statesmen, heroes and ordinary Joes we had seen, Dubya was the best. The oft-cited defects of animatronic technology, the fact that it makes characters seem stiff and only intermittently lifelike, were no problem. Dubya was born to the medium…(5)

And in the process of writing this piece a report on the rebuilding of New Orleans following the unthinkable destruction wrought by Hurricane Katrina in *The Observer* newspaper echoed something I'd heard on the news a few days previous:

As images of Katrina start to fade, tourists will return. With the projects razed and criminals gone, big business will also return. In place of slums will be condos and cluster homes; where the Lower Ninth stood, golf courses. Mayor Nagin has even proposed a law permitting casinos in most hotels. Ten years from now, if Nagin has his way, New Orleans may be Las Vegas South.(6)

A society occupied, remodelled and (re)animated as an entertainment complex.

The deliberate lack of critical distance in the experience of the McCarthys' own theme park manifests a world without an exit strategy and a confusion of positions, between the viewer and the viewed. It finds its parallel in Stephanie Rosenthal's catalogue essay description of how Paul McCarthy's work tests the boundaries of the physical body to the point of dissolution. She constructs a metaphor between McCarthy's work as a physical body in relationship to, comparable to, the architecture of an idiosyncratic house:

> This house metaphor is, to be sure, only correct when one does not think of an ordinary house, but rather [one] with tilted floors, with holes in the floors and ceilings, and without a roof, so that the rain falls through all the levels. The water is then pumped back up from the bottom of the house and shot back in under high pressure through the windows and other openings.(7)

It is precisely dissolution between interior and exterior that VALIE EXPORT is concerned with in her feature length film *Invisible Adversaries* (Unsichtbare Gegner, 1978). The film's protagonist – an artist named Anna – enacts this dissolution: (her) perception, knowledge, the/her body, city, by extension the state, are thrown into a nexus of relationships where mediation – the *mediated* self – and apparent mental instability, map onto each other. As in *Caribbean Pirates*, the linear arrangement of space and time collapses, though the moral disintegration that accompanies McCarthy's installation instead, in *Invisible Adversaries*, becomes the structured examination of a political and social condition. VALIE EXPORT does not so much occupy and animate the forms of mass media (mass entertainment) as demonstrate the media's occupation of the world at large. The film in this sense forms an unlikely (historical) bridge between the work of Paul McCarthy and that of Catherine Sullivan.

The premise is this: Anna is convinced of having heard radio announcements amidst a string of national and international headlines, that the world has been invaded – and people occupied – by invisible aliens called Hyksos that control behaviour. Whether this is insight or delusion remains ambiguous. Anna is VALIE EXPORT's avatar. Her practice is that of VALIE EXPORT, the actual artist's works appearing in the film as those of Anna. A discussion of the film and its strategies is also a discussion of VALIE EXPORT's practice, that is here presented as both precipitating, and as the symptom of, an obsessive, sometimes visionary spiral. Anna obsessively documents herself and her surroundings, her relationship/s; she photographs herself naked, emulating the poses of classical paintings in modern dress with everyday objects, wraps her body around street furniture, into corners, mediates a conversation with her lover using video monitors, makes video recordings of other women speaking, fixes her own shadow, photographs her own excrement, speaks her lover's name into a Dictaphone, makes herself a moustache from her pubic hair, sees a row of cardboard cut-out figures on a balustrade in a city square and falls down after circling them, herself become a two-dimensional image. Anna is seen photographing a building being torn down at the same time as developing its image in her darkroom. Two men walk down the street wearing sandwich boards made of mirrors, she looks at herself in a mirror at home and her reflection has a life of its own. A man is lying down in the middle of a road, slowly licking the tarmac.

Sound splits from image: a man's guttural, growling voice is heard over a photograph of a woman's vagina (as in VALIE EXPORT's short film *Mann & Frau & Animal* (1973)), the turning pages of a book sound like a machine gun. As Anna's partner is seen in an absurdist, Kafkaesque altercation with a parking attendant, we see close-up shots of salami being sliced until it is revealed that Peter is telling her this story as she prepares dinner. Their conversation descends into an argument that is apparently infectious. Everyone, everywhere across the city is arguing. War footage of running street battles, ravaged cities. The personal is utterly interconnected with the political.

Invisible Adversaries' complex balance of occupations is figured in the mind, the body and in the (perceived) social system. Shots of modern-day Vienna are accompanied by a voiceover that describes the city's history as one of 'oblivion and treason':

> In wickedness and brutality, population and authorities are as one. The cultural climate of the Second Republic has heightened this continuum of corruption by its

banality. The banality of evil is not Viennese dirty washing, but its very face. The Viennese golden heart, beating faster for a dog than for an artist, has been the death of many. If you're creative in Vienna the police suspects you.

A history of Viennese architecture ensues, with a list of the abuses conducted by the state on its architects. A disrobed, faceless priest is seen on a sun lounger masturbating, echoed later in the film when Anna leaves her doctor's and, walking home, passes a number of single men, 'police cadets', masturbating in doorways and stairwells.

Anna and Peter have a heated conversation over lunch. Peter insists upon the dominance of a socio-political system that is out of individuals' control, of which they are but a side effect. Anna asserts personal responsibility. This is the trajectory that *Invisible Adversaries* tracks: occupation against independence, agency against articulation. The film's metaphoric, surrealist coda details the Hyksos' greatest threat – the reduction of individuals to automata, occupation not as the opening (or the animation) of a form, but as depoliticising automation.

Instead of witnessing the whole of an action that has taken place over time, as we do in McCarthy's *Pirate Party*, *Invisible Adversaries* presents an action with its psycho-symbolic visual correlative, or simultaneously (inseparably), with its document. Anna's crisis, what plays upon (and is an extension of) her own nervous system, is VALIE EXPORT's enquiry. It turns upon questions of agency – intent, action/inaction, responsibility – and of systems played out and back upon themselves. Transgression, in this context, is not the act of documenting, but of transcending the document; the film's final image a photograph ripped in two.

Catherine Sullivan's *The Chittendens* (2005) was, ironically enough, first shown in Vienna, at Secession. It is a six-screen video work. Like McCarthy's installation, its exhibition in London (at Tate Modern where I saw it) was a reordering of its first manifestation. The piece comprised two projection rooms. An antechamber contained an elliptical projection screen and a second room that was long and relatively narrow had screens on three sides. The audience completed the rectangle on the fourth side, seated on benches facing three projection screens, with one screen on each of the short ends of

Invisible Adversaries VALIE EXPORT (1998)
Courtesy the artist/Cinenova, London/127

the room so that the experience was of confronting the proscenium arch, or at least the (projected) performance space (and the wings) of a theatrical stage. Unlike McCarthy's belligerently positioned projections with their overlaps, overhangs and angles *The Chittendens'* images are pristinely aligned, fitting their screens perfectly, signalling the work's acute structure. It is a complex work, the full exegesis of which is not my intent here other than at some points of intersection with *Caribbean Pirates* and *Invisible Adversaries*. Like Paul McCarthy, Catherine Sullivan too is interested in the sea, its alternative sets of rules, in the past and the present, occupation and animation, the occupation and animation of these things.

In the antechamber, on an oval screen, a naval Captain in historical uniform is seen at sea, approaching an island. The scene is idyllic: blue sea, foliage, smooth camera movement and the gentle swell of the ocean are matched by a lyrical soundtrack and describe each other. The Captain looks through his telescope towards the island with its lighthouse and we see what he sees. A woman, also in period dress, is rocking backwards and forwards on the cliff, like a neurotic siren. People dressed in pure white overalls signify routine and seem to be going about their daily work. The captain walks amongst these workers, the two not acknowledging each other as if they inhabit parallel spaces in parallel time zones. The Captain as a sign of hierarchy, the workers of the communal, preface and summarise the work's concerns: the co-existence of contrasting (social) systems.

In the main room, the coordination of sound, action and image across the four sections of the five-screen work is specific, choreographed to direct the gaze and to work symphonically, in stark contrast to the consistent, chaotic immersion of *Caribbean Pirates*. Sean Griffin's commissioned score moves from lyrical ballad to broken, industrial repetitions. Catherine Sullivan's performers occupy period and contemporary dress, sometimes a hybrid of the two, sometimes simultaneously, the same actor performing the same actions in and 'out' of costume, superimposed onto each other. They move mechanically, trapped in slapstick loops, expressive, repetitious, hysterical, abstracted, neurotic. A male voice talks about ancient watches that start to tick again, like the woken dead. Instead of ransacking a film set or exploring a city besieged by unseen invaders, *The Chittendens* occupies semi-derelict, half-furnished ex-insurance company offices, from which the piece borrows its title. The work's prologue maps its divisions

(and differences) of labour onto them both by association and through the animated bodies of its surrealist, dysfunctional workforce.

It is no coincidence that Catherine Sullivan uses the verb 'to animate' throughout her own description of the piece (published to accompany the exhibition) in which process is critical. Actors were ascribed 14 'attitudes', derived by the artist from her interaction with them. Each of these could, by her, then be:

- minimised or maximised in terms of dramatic stakes
- reduced or expanded in physical form
- abbreviated or extended in terms of time(8)

She goes on, 'The attitudes and their treatments were then assigned to a series of numeric patterns which could be executed rhythmically at multiple tempo.' The relationship between artist and performer occurs within and is regulated by a set of fixed terms. The performer's body, to the limit of its possibility, is mechanised. Psychological interaction becomes the subject of a system that foregoes naturalism, extenuating its own instance into stylised movement and (generally abstract) sound. In *Invisible Adversaries* Anna collapses twice, her body given over to the physical manifestation of her psychological condition. In *The Chittendens* this loss of control is harnessed and styled into artifice, while in McCarthy's *Pirate Party* physical abandon is a key function of the performers' – and by implication the viewers' – collusion in moral decline. In each case it marks a deliberate removal of the body from normative patterns of behaviour. In each work, the relationship between (self) expression and the body articulates central theses about (self) control, variously unpicking, or re-describing, the/our social and moral fabric by eliding realism with strategies derived from or in metaphorical relation to the abstracts of animation.

Catherine Sullivan details how her reading of Thorstein Veblen's *The Theory of the Leisure Class* (1899) threads its way into *The Chittendens*. Veblen constructs the 'leisure class' as a social grouping that emerges during the development of social relationships to ownership – during the 'unexplained' transition from 'peaceable savage' (no class divisions, simple social structures uninformed by private ownership) to 'predatory barbarian' ('defined by the maintenance of wealth and ownership acquired by unceasing force and predatory habit').(9) Industrial capitalism is equated with the high barbarian,

The Chittendens Catherine Sullivan (2005)
Courtesy the artist/Metro Pictures, New York/129

and labour, in this context, becomes linked to exploitation, to the power of and control over animate things – ultimately, other people. Paul McCarthy's First Mate. Peter's system over Anna's personal responsibility. Against repression, *The Chittendens* is a chorus of neurotic habits, a multitude of classes occupied and venting, the inverse of the society from which Anna removes herself, engaged in a kind of automation, of animation, that is profoundly connected to a kind of psychotic liberation.

In the opening paragraph of his essay *Will the Monster Eat the Film?*, a dossier of artist-animators' practice between 1980–94 in the context of increasingly industrialised opportunities for the form, Simon Pummell evokes *Alien*^{3}:

> In the Hollywood blockbuster *Alien*^{3}... the monster eats all the characters the viewer can identify with or be interested in (excepting the heroine Ripley) in the first third of the film. ...the real thriller if whether the monster will eat the narrative before it resolves itself in a classical narrative fashion. It represents cinema teetering between the narrative... of classical cinema and the plastic spectacle (the monster) of digital and special fx cinema; in fact the cinema of animation.(10)

He concludes that 'the forms traditionally used to describe the monstrous... the magic... the marginal, childish and grotesque... are being used more and more to describe our experience as post modern subjects.'(11)

Whether or not anyone wants to be a 'post modern subject', it is not so much the way we are being described that feels at stake, but the ways in which we are behaving that have become monstrous, magical, marginal, childish and grotesque. And that these things are revealed through animation as strategy, and animation as metaphor, rather than masked by its complicity with illusion, fantasy or escape. Oskar Fischinger refused to be complicit in the macabre carnival of Disney's industrialised workplace; there is no little irony in that his contract was finally terminated on Hallow'een.

Endnotes

1 Welchman, John, 'First Mate's Bloody Flux', *Paul McCarthy LaLa Land Parody Paradise*, Rosenthal, Stephanie, ed., Haus der Kunst, Munich, 2005, p192

2 http://disneyland.disney.go.com/disneyland/en_US/parks/attractions/detail?name= PiratesOfTheCaribbeanAttractionPage

3 'McCarthy's studio becomes more and more a constructed mimicry of a Hollywood film production company with no intention of making legitimate "Hollywood films."', Rosenthal, Stephanie, 'How to Use a Failure', *Paul McCarthy LaLa Land Parody Paradise*, op. cit., p136

4 Ibid, p196

5 Hickey, Dave, 'Welcome to Dreamsville', *Vanity Fair*, August 2005, no. 540, p129

6 Cohn, Nick, 'The Day the Music Died', *The Observer Review*, 15 January 2006, p6

7 Rosenthal, Stephanie, op. cit., p130

8 Sullivan, Catherine, '*The Chittendens*', *Catherine Sullivan The Chittendens*, Revolver, 2005, p16

9 Ibid, p23

10 Pummell, Simon, 'Will the Monster Eat the Film? or The Redefinition of British Animation 1980–1994', O'Pray, Michael, ed., *The British Avant-Garde Film 1926 to 1995*, University of Luton Press, 1996, p299

11 Ibid, p313

WHO I AM
AND
WHAT I WANT

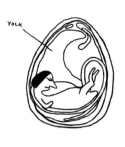

YOLK

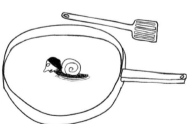

A FILM BY
CHRIS SHEPHERD
DAVID SHRIGLEY

Curating *The Animators*
Angela Kingston

The Animators was a touring gallery exhibition which arose from initial research commissioned by animate! The exhibition included work by Ann Course, Katy Dove, Simon Faithfull, Dryden Goodwin, Paul Morrison, Vong Phaophanit & Claire Oboussier and took place at Angel Row Gallery, Nottingham (the commissioning venue); SPACEX, Exeter and Ferens Art Gallery, Hull during 2005–2006.

The exhibition seemed at first to be based on a quite simple premise. It would look at one particular artform: animation, in the context of a surge in artists using animation techniques. Computer software packages now make it possible to work freely with digital imagery, and artists have been quick to seize on the increased potential that exists to make still images move.

When taking on the task of curating this exhibition, I found a wider field available to me than I had first thought. The term animation has recently expanded to incorporate all manner of real-time film footage that has been 'messed about with'. We usually think of animations in terms of cartoons that have been drawn or of models moved frame-by-frame, but animation now includes 'normal' films which have been intensively reworked with rapid edits and cuts, repeats and reversals, speedings-up and slowings-down, collage effects and digital manipulations.

Artists, who tend to work experimentally with whatever medium they use, now often find their films categorised as animations, and this can come as a surprise. For my part, researching this exhibition involved remembering artists' films that I was already very interested in and recognising them as animations. And of course I also sought out animations by artists that I had previously been unaware of.

One strong memory was of a film by the painter Paul Morrison, which I came across as an unexpected part of an exhibition of paintings by him.(1) His paintings (and also his

136/*Acrospire* Paul Morrison (2005). Courtesy of Alison Jacques Gallery, London

screenprints) juxtapose different ways of depicting the landscape, borrowing from cartoons, botanical illustrations, 'old master' prints and other sources. The various elements are rendered as stark black-on-white silhouettes and there are strange shifts in scale (a fern can be as tall as a fir tree). When I met Paul Morrison, he explained that he approaches the process of picturemaking in filmmaking terms: editing and cropping, zooming and panning, for example. It seemed natural to him to start to work with film itself.

Paul Morrison's films are, like his paintings and prints, reworkings of existing depictions of the landscape, and this time his imagery is taken from feature films. *Acrospire* (2005), which was included in *The Animators*, splices together footage of woods and open water taken from such diverse movies as Walt Disney's *Snow White and the Seven Dwarfs* (1937), Tarkovsky's *Andrei Roublev* (1966) and the British cult thriller *The Black Windmill* (1974). As with his paintings, Paul Morrison has rendered everything in black and white.

The artist's treatment of this material is very curious. Rivers appear to travel in both directions at once; footage of dark and brooding clouds has been set into reverse, and the clouds roll back in on themselves and disappear; a will-o'-the-wisp is sucked with rapid force into the base of a tree. It is as if nature is siphoning back its offerings. Interspersed with this, however, are some cartoon amoebic life forms that quiver and burst, and some Disney-style watery ripples and swirling leaves. For the soundtrack, Paul Morrison has sampled the dubbed-in cinema sound effects of howling wind and glugging water.

There is a halting quality to *Acrospire*, too. Paul Morrison has not massaged the different films seamlessly into one another. A subtle disjointedness in the edits and the restless shifts from place to place and between film genres keep returning you to yourself, conscious again of standing in a darkened space, watching the animation.

Ann Course is, by contrast, an animator in the most traditional sense, first making drawings that she then sets in motion using a computer. These drawings are rapidly executed and her animation of them is jagged and unruly. Crude and rude, her images erupt like expletives onto the screen: there are 'explicit sexual fantasies, mutilation scenes, grotesque faces, ridiculous transformations and the occasional line or two of

cryptic text'.(2) Yet her animations are as funny as they are brutal. This is partly because they involve us in what one writer has described as 'the collective memory of cartoons – an animistic world of fiction laden with violence, deep psychological impulses and the recollection of childhood.'(3) Ann Course's wincingly hilarious scenes are *Tom and Jerry* made adult and more shameful.

It's not only the content of this work that stirs us, but also the animation itself. She is, she says, 'amazed at what you can get away with'. She will lay down one image and follow it with another that is quite different. Gaping-wide edits leave us scrambling to follow the action and her train of thought, and yet an overarching, breathless momentum will take us along with it all. On the other hand, short sequences that she does animate are repeated rather teasingly, for our pleasure perhaps, and to reinforce a mood or a loose sense of narrative – and also, more curiously, to taunt us with the very illusion of apparent movement within animations.

The haunting, halting quality of Paul Morrison's film; the teasing stop-start effect of Ann Course's; I was seeing other artists' animations, too, which likewise have a strange and somehow 'wrong' type of movement and temporality. It seemed to me that animations by artists very often communicate a quality of stillness.(4)

This subtle aspect of the films needed to be given an airing, and I approached Mark Hutchinson, an artist and writer, and asked him to contribute an essay about stillness to the project. In the resulting text he considers photography and painting, and describes how different types of stillness attach to these forms: the sitter posing stock-still for the painter or photographer; the literal stillness of the resulting image; the contemplative stillness of the viewer. On the other hand, the very stillness of an image can be the focus of mental un-stillness: it 'leave[s] a greater space for the exploration and interpretation of the viewer', giving rise to 'critical activity' rather than 'intellectual passivity'. And what is more, both paintings and photographs result from processes of observation and decision-making: they are accumulations of time, rather than being truly static.

A film, Mark Hutchinson writes, is self-evidently concerned with movement; yet it is, paradoxically, made of stills. These are, however, made automatically and mechanically: the camera is positioned, the button is pressed and the film rolls. Animation has creative

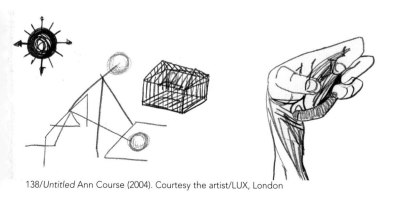
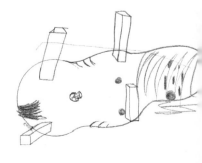

138/*Untitled* Ann Course (2004). Courtesy the artist/LUX, London

and critical potential, he argues, because it brings 'the constructions of picturemaking into the making of each still'. As a marriage of the still and the moving, it 'presents the possibility of interrupting or analysing both the temporal flow of film and the spatial stillness of pictures'.(5)

Simon Faithfull is a third artist who became a crucial part of *The Animators*. He contributed a remarkably simple animation that attests to what Mark Hutchinson has identified here. *Dog Breathing*, which depicts a dog curled up asleep, was made using a Palm Pilot (a simple, hand-held, digital device). Just eight drawn outlines of a dog make up the animation, which is seen in a continuous loop: we see the uneven rise and fall of the dog's chest, and the occasional slight movements of its muzzle, as if dreaming. The artist instructed that his animation should be installed in the gallery 'in exactly the kind of place where a dog would go and lie down to sleep'. It is a paradigm piece of exquisite simplicity in which everything leads to the compulsion of seeing life in this animation (a word derived from *animare*, Latin for filling with breath and life).

However, in *Dog Breathing* the animation is again tenuous; it is deliberately intermittent and slight. The obvious stillness of the outline drawings throws us back once more on ourselves; yet in almost the same moment, the subtle movement enraptures us, and takes us along with it, almost without us being able to help it. To use Mark Hutchinson's words, the 'spatial stillness' is made to have a curious relationship with the 'temporal flow'.

Stillness became a quality that I actively looked for in the selection of the remaining animations for the exhibition. But on an entirely practical note, I was conscious of the difficulties that arise when films are projected in galleries. What do you do with the spaces between the screens? And there is the problem, too, of sound spilling from exhibit to exhibit and merging into a cacophony. The simple solution was to show other kinds of artworks amongst the animations, so that the sets of equipment would be at a helpful distance from each other. All the artists in *The Animators*, therefore, needed also to be painters or sculptors or photographers and so on. By mixing their different approaches in the exhibition, there was the bonus of witnessing each artist's creative thumbprint across the different artforms.

A series of 12 black and white screenprints of fantastical landscapes by Paul Morrison,

Dog Breathing Simon Faithfull (2005). *Courtesy the artist*/139

called *Black Dahlias*, was shown at Angel Row Gallery and Ferens Art Gallery near a darkened booth in which his animation *Acrospire* was playing (at SPACEX, the nature of the gallery spaces meant that we decided to stage *The Animators* straightforwardly, as an animation-only exhibition). In another booth there was a programme of animations by Ann Course: nearby were her sculptures in clay, rubber, metal and stained glass, and her screenprints. There were echoes of images in her animations – boots, buckets, pies, sexually suggestive shapes – and it was possible to see her preoccupations at work within a surprising range of media, still and moving.

Simon Faithfull worked with Jim Waters, project manager of *The Animators*, to have a sign fabricated with a pixilated drawing on it by Simon of an arrow pointing upwards, together with the word 'sky'. They arranged for this sign to be taken out into the street and held aloft in much the way of signs that advertise golf sales or pizza restaurants. In between times, the sign rested in the gallery as an exhibit, together with photographs that revealed its 'life' (its animation) out on the street.

There was a programme of eight animations by Katy Dove and this was seen alongside a selection of her drawings, watercolour paintings and screenprints. The relationship between these different artworks was immediately apparent. To create her animations, she makes hundreds of coloured drawings, some of them stream of consciousness, others more planned: she then scans a selection into a computer and animates them. Groups of shapes drift about on the screen, disappearing for a while and then reappearing. The soundtracks, too, are meandering and repetitive.

Her two-dimensional works on paper involve subtle reiterations of abstract shapes. The artist sees her two-dimensional pieces as existing independently, however; the forms and shapes in these works do not necessarily cross into her animations.

Throughout her work, Katy Dove evokes an untethered and daydreaming state of mind – into which something more shadowy and menacing occasionally drifts. In the animation *You* (2002), there are dancing hearts, flowers and rainbows, and cascading ribbons, leaves and feathers; intermittently, however, disquieting shapes with blank eyes loom into view.

140/*You* Katy Dove (2002). Courtesy the artist

There is a magical quality to Katy Dove's animations, a sense of wonder at the simple miracle of seeing these innocently hand-drawn shapes move. Yet a sense of stillness pervades this artist's animations, too. We recognise it as the simple and necessary corollary of the movement – and we watch for it in the stately yet erratic movement of the shapes.

In a third adjoining gallery, Dryden Goodwin's looped 16mm film *Two Thousand and Three* was installed. This comprises 2003 frames, each of which is a still image of a different individual on an anti-war march. The artist captured the images frame-by-frame using a movie camera. When the film is seen running through a projector, individual faces appear in a rapid and jerky succession. But strangely, sometimes a single head appears to turn, and at other times an individual seems to pass by. The artist has animated together the people in the crowd, in a process that occurred then and there, inside the camera. To one side, there were strips of the same film on a light-box, and we were invited to scrutinise the utter stillness of the celluloid frames. Here, the experience of 'spatial stillness' was prised apart from that of 'temporal flow' and the paradox of film as moving stillness was laid bare.

Dryden Goodwin also exhibited *Cradle* (2002), a series of still photographs he took of people unawares on the streets. Once they were developed and enlarged, he scratched lines into the photographs, creating net-like forms that appear to entrap the faces of his subjects. An act of connection and intrusion has happened twice: when the photographs were taken and when the scratches were made.

But the point is of course that we don't really experience the photographs, paintings and sculptures as static (if they interest and move us, that is). Mark Hutchinson's essay, as I've mentioned earlier, describes how still images can give rise to mental activity, and how they also represent accumulations of time – which we as viewers reactivate, perhaps.

I think it is also interesting to reflect on how artists tend to choose the most inert and passive materials – think of blank paper and lumpen clay.(6) They then work with these substances in such a way that when we then look at what they have made, we invest those same, worked, materials with a curious kind of 'life'. This we perceive not just cerebrally, but with our whole bodies, too.

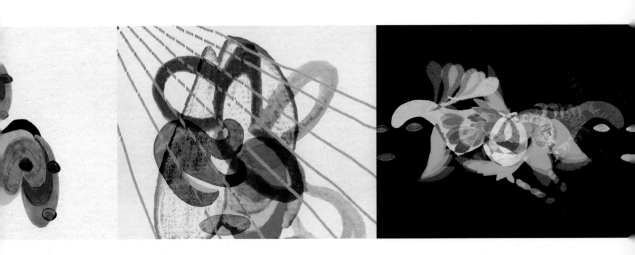

When we look at Dryden Goodwin's *Cradle*, we re-enact the making of the work – the snatching of the photograph, the passionate scorings into the faces of the strangers – and we also occupy the place of the people unknown to the artist reached from across the void in this curious way. If at this moment of recognition we had sensors connected to our hands and faces, they would register a flicker of activity. When we look at Ann Course's clay pies (*You, Me, Them*, 2004), we smile at their homemade quality and perverse ordinariness – and by smiling, we seem to be *smiling back at them*. We have caught their mood.

These are examples of what David Maclagan calls the 'creative response' to art, which he describes as having an 'embodied nature'. He writes, about the act of looking at and writing about art:

> … aesthetic responses are 'performed'… This performance is an internal one, when we rehearse our responses inwardly to a greater or lesser extent, and it is also an external one once the writing of them is involved … In practice the two interact: I may not yet know what I feel until I put it into words.(7)

And what is particularly interesting in this context is how frequently writers, when they are discussing sculpture, painting and photography, describe themselves as being *animated* by these artforms. Once I began to research this exhibition, I stumbled across many examples of this. Here is perhaps the best instance of all, by Roland Barthes, in which he is describing the feelings he has when, after seeing a great many indifferent photographs, one excites him:

> In this glum desert, suddenly a specific photograph reaches me; it animates me and I animate it. So that is how I must name the attraction which makes it exist: an *animation*. The photograph itself is in no way animated (I do not believe in 'lifelike' photographs), but it animates me: this is what creates every adventure.(8)

This became the overarching claim of *The Animators*: that the artists are animators not only of frames of film but also of paper, ink, clay and other basic materials.

Vong Phaophanit exhibited a series of sculptures in *The Animators* in which he took commonplace objects and subjected them to obsessive processes that alter their nature and presence. In *Stratified Figures* (2004–05), he repeatedly dipped ornamental porcelain

142/*England and Poland* Vong Phaophanit and Claire Oboussier (2005). Courtesy the artists

characters into melted wax, which has hardened to form strange accretions. The figures have been all but obliterated by this, and now sport protuberances that are by turns comic and phantasmic.

In other sculptures, Vong Phaophanit has drilled thousands of frenzied holes into a child's plastic chair, a skateboard and a trunk, reaching the point where the objects can take no more. On the verge of disintegration, they started to bend in our hands as we cradled them out of their boxes and installed them on the plinths.

Both the dipped and drilled sculptures seem to suggest that the attention we pay to certain things can overload their meaning to the point of obscurity, or that our gaze is somehow corrosive. The drilled sculptures in particular are perhaps the exception that proves the rule: husks of objects with their materiality extracted from them, at a precarious stage of deathly decay.(9) If the objects have a new 'life' as sculptures, it is a ghostly one.

Very recently, Vong Phaophanit started to make animations with his longtime collaborator Claire Oboussier,(10) an example of which they exhibited for the first time in *The Animators*. Their animation *England and Poland* (2005) also involves the process of extraction. They have taken a televised football match and digitally removed the object at the centre of the activity – the football. It has become a game of 'spot the ball', and a ballet emerges in which the players seem entranced and strangely liberated.

Watching *England and Poland*, my gaze constantly drifts away from the television on which this animation is being played. The loss of the ball as the centre of attention seems to cause my eyes to wander away from the action. After a short while, I no longer hear the commentary and I have lost my focus. Here, too, I experience a state of reverie and stillness amongst all the movement.

A version of this essay appears in a book published by Angel Row Gallery in 2006 that documents and discusses *The Animators*.

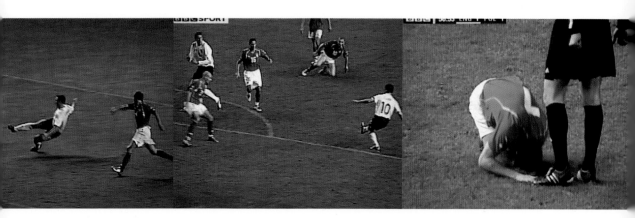

Endnotes

1 aspreyjacques, London, 2002

2 Edwin Carels, www.luxonline.com, 2005

3 Christov-Bakargiev, Carolyn, *Animations*, Kunst-Werke Institute for Contemporary Art, Berlin, 2003, p14

4 See also Curtis, David, *Art and Animation*, Channel 4 Television, 1999, p16

5 *The Animators*, exhibition catalogue published by Angel Row Gallery, Nottingham, 2006

6 This was pointed out to me by the sculptor Paul Carter during a conversation in autumn 2002, when he went as far as saying that artists seem to have consistently chosen the most boring materials to work with.

7 Maclagan, David, *Psychological Aesthetics: Painting, Feeling and Making Sense*, Jessica Kingsley Publishers, 2005, p115

8 Barthes, Roland, (translated by Richard Howard,) *Camera Lucida*, Vintage, 2000, p20 (the emphasis is in the original). I am grateful to artist-animator Katy Shepherd for drawing my attention to this extract.

9 A member of the public made this observation during a discussion of *The Animators*.

10 *The Animators* also included a sculpture by Claire Oboussier, *Abode* (2000), in which she also worked with an existing object, a birdcage. This had had some of its wires cut and been inverted, to 'release' an insect-like creature.

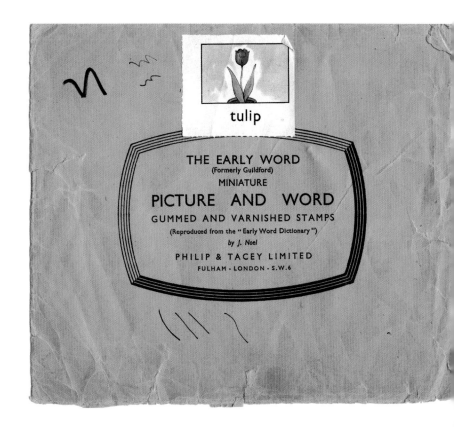

grass   jar   van

ink   idol   tree

iron   jewel   muff

jam   jug   kettle

catch   picture   read   over

swing   jump   under   mother

cake   up   make   children

girl   shoe   farm   father

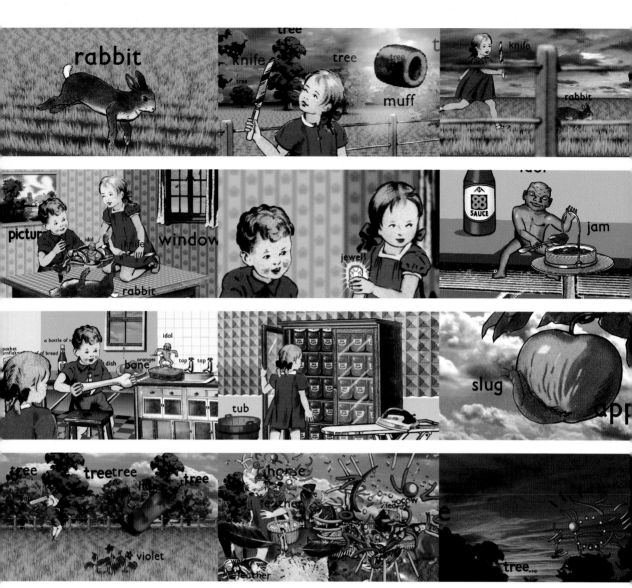

the *animate!* book

Further Information

Information on animate! including all of the works produced through the project and the ongoing commissioning programme can be found at www.animateonline.org

The animate! project is produced by Finetake www.finetake.co.uk

animate! is funded by Arts Council England www.artscouncil.org.uk and Channel 4 www.channel4.com

All the works commissioned by animate! are distributed by LUX www.lux.org.uk

Contributors

Dick Arnall is an independent film producer, founder in 1967 of the UK's first international animation festival, director of Finetake Limited, and producer of the animate! project.

Edwin Carels works as a programmer and curator for the IFFR (International Film Festival Rotterdam), and as head of the film and media department of the MuHKA (Museum of Contemporary Art Antwerp).

Benjamin Cook is director of LUX, London.

Eileen Daly is a freelance book editor.

Gareth Evans is a writer and independent film/events programmer. He works on the film pages of *Time Out* London and edits the independent moving image journal *Vertigo* (www.vertigomagazine.co.uk).

Angela Kingston is an independent visual arts curator and writer. She is currently curating an exhibition called *Fairy Tale* which will open at The New Art Gallery Walsall.

Mike Sperlinger is a freelance writer and assistant director of LUX, London.

Gary Thomas is head of moving image, Arts Council England.

Ian White is adjunct film curator for Whitechapel Gallery, London, a freelance curator, writer and artist.

Exposure

a film by Peter Collis

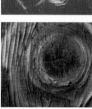

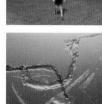

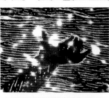

1993
Winter Trees Sarah Downes
Museum of Stolen Souls Chris Elliott
Biogenesis William Latham

1994
What She Wants
Ruth Lingford
Stressed Karen Kelly
Save Me Stuart Hilton
Jumping Joan Petra Freeman
Jukebox Run Wrake
His Comedy Paul Bush
End of Restriction
Robert Bradbrook
Within/Without
Benita Raphan

1995
Scrutiny Ian Cross
Heliocentrum Richard Wright
& Jason White
15th February Tim Webb

1996
Sunset Strip Kayla Parker
Go West Young Man Keith Piper
Crimplene Michelle Salamon

1997
Withdrawal George Barber
SKZCP Riccardo Iacono
Miles from Anywhere Gary Carpenter
Feeling My Way Jonathan Hodgson
3 Ways to Go Sarah Cox

List of *animate!* Commissions
1991-2007

animate!

Full details and credit information
for all commissions can be found
at www.animateonline.org

animate! title sequence

1991
Cowboys (Murder)
Phil Mulloy

1992
Spirit of Place Oliver Harrison
Soho Square Mario Cavalli
Naked Yasmine Ramli
Cage of Flame Kayla Parker

List of *animate!* Commissions 1991-2007

Miles from Anywh

ROLL 2 - SHOT 1   9.8.96
BIG ROCK - NEAR MALHAM COVE.
THE SUN WAS RISING. COLOUR TEMP.
WILL CHANGE.   MOVING AROUND THE
ROCK - WILL THE DIFFERENT SHADOWS
SHOW ?

ROLL 2 - SHOT 2   9.8.96
FACE OF MALHAM COVE.
LIGHT READINGS SEEMED OVER.
INSTEAD OF ZOOMING OUT, I STEPPED
BACK.

ROLL 2 - SHOT 3   9.8.96
LIMESTONE PAVEMENT
TREACHEROUS ! SHOT AT A 45° ANGLE.
SOMEONE SAID 'ANIMATION' IN FRENCH '.

WONDERING IF THE CYCLE WILL
SHOW OF ME WALKING BACK
AND FORTH.

ROLL 2 - SHOT 4   9.8.96
ABORTED - BARBED WIRE
TOO MUCH BACKLIGHT, TOO HIGH UP.
FOCUS TRICKY.

ROLL 2 - SHOT 5   9.8.96
ROUGH STONE PATH, MALHAM.
200 FT. UP & DOWN 200 FT ZOOM
THEN SG F WHICH ARE PROBABLY
OUT OF FOCUS.   VERY LOW LIGHT

ROLL 2 - SHOT 6 9.8.96
MALHAM - BARBED WIRE
SHOOTING INTO THE SKY COULD
COMPLICATE EXPOSURE. HAD TO
ZOOM OUT DUE TO ROCKY VERGE.
CHASED BY FLIES.   (LOOK FOR DUST
ON CLOTHES)

ROLL 2 - SHOT 7   9.8.96
LONG GRASS - MALHAM.
I'M NOT SURE IF ALL THE DIFFERENT
ANGLES / DIRECTIONS OF GRASS WILL
WORK CONSECUTIVELY.
COWS ARE FINDING ME VERY
INTERESTING

MPA
M 0919740   POSTED
ROLL 2   A.M. 9.8.96
             FOR 11.30 POST

ROLL 3 - SHOT 1   10.8.96
SCREE - GORDALE SCAR, MALHAM.
USED SAME SIZED ROCKS & ZOOM
OUT / IN, MAY LOOK LIKE A PROGRESSION
TO DIFFERENTLY ERODED ROCKS.
THE MOST ACTIVE SHOOT SO FAR   BACKWARDS!

ROLL 3 - SHOT 2   10.8.96
GORDALE SCAR , MALHAM.
SHOT FROM FAR WITH FULL ZOOM.
SAT DOWN. THE LEAST ACTIVE SHOT
SO FAR.   IMPRESSION OF SPEED

ROLL 3 - SHOT 3   10.8.96
GORDALE SCAR - CLOSE UP
CRACKS AND JUTTING OUT BITS.
MORE INTERESTING YELLOW & LICHEN.
MOVED?

ROLL 3 - SHOT 4   10.8.96
THISTLES - Nr. GORDALE
AERIAL VIEW WITH SLIGHT ROTATION
TOWARDS END OF SHOT.

ROLL 3 - SHOT 5 10.8.96
LIMESTONE WALL, MALHAM.
CONCENTRATED ON NEGATIVE SPACES.
CONSTRUCTION OF THE WALL BECAME
MORE REGULAR AS I WENT ALONG.
ZOOM PIXILATION ACROSS WALL
AT END.

ROLL 3 - SHOT 6 10.8.96.
PATH TO MALHAM COVE.
VERY LOW LIGHT.- 28 dL.
STARTED IN CLOSE & ZOOM
OUT.   DAN TOOK PROD. STILLS

ROLL 3 - SHOT 7   10.8.96.
BROOK ADJ PATH.
PROBABLY OUT OF FILM. TOOK
100 F. ANYWAY. NO LIGHT
READING.

M 0919739   ROLL 3
ROLL 3   POSTED 11.8.96
             FOR SUNDAY POST.

ROLL 4 - SHOT 1   11.8.96
MOSSY FACE - GORDALE SCAR.
LOADS OF YELLOW STUFF. LOW LIGHT
(F2 - 2.8) BUT STEADY. FAST PULL
OUT TOWARDS END.

ROLL 4 - SHOT 2   11.8.96
LIMESTONE - Nr MALHAM TARN.
HORIZONTAL CRACKS AND SURFACE
MARKS. WIERD WHITE CIRCLES, ALMOST
LIKE FOSSILS . ENDS WITH TENDRILLY
MOSS. (ABOUT 9 ft.)

ROLL 4 - SHOT 3   11.8.96
CATTLE GRID - MALHAM
STARTED WITH A
PATTERN, BUT THOUGHT THE END
ONES WOULD BE OBVIOUSLY REPEATED
SO SWITCHED TO   , THE SLATS
WERE DIFFERENT DISTANCES APART
(SLIGHTLY) SO A 'PULSE' SHOULD
SHOW. DISTURBED BY CARS

ROLL 4 - SHOT 4   11.8.96.
WIRE FENCE - Nr. MALHAM
JOINS IN WEAVE LOOK LIKE A
FIST. SHEEP IN THE BACKGROUND
MAY PIXILATE.

ROLL 4 - SHOT 5   11.8.96
LIMESTONE PAVEMENT - MALHAM
YELLOWER TODAY. FILMED GRYKES

OPENING AND CLOSING. 200 F C/U,
150 F. ZOOM OUT, 100 F. WIDE.
DAN DID PORTRAITS OF ME HERE

ROLL 4 - SHOT 6   11.8.96.
LIMESTONE PAVEMENT WITH GRASS.
TWO TEXTURES. VERY LITTLE REGISTRATION
IF ANY. HARD TO KEEP ORIENTATION
THE SAME SO SHADOWS SHOULD BE
WILD.

ROLL 4 - SHOT 6   12.8.96
BUSH IN MALHAM VILLAGE.
7:30 a.m. REDS & GREENS.
WENT RIGHT INTO SUBJECT AT LAST
50 F. CAMERA MIGHT LOOK LIKE ITS
BEING ATTACKED

ROLL 4 - SHOT 7   12.8.96
PILE OF BRANCHES - THE WEETS
                   SD 924 636
SUDDEN ZOOM IN AT F5. 180 - 200

film
Gary Carpenter

The animate! Book DVD

DVD contains a selection of animate! works chosen by Dick Arnall and Gareth Evans

Contents

That's Nothin' from Cowboys Phil Mulloy (1991, 3 min)
One film from a series of six, three-minute films which comment on contemporary values through a reinterpretation of the myths of the old Wild West. Mulloy's witty and acerbic fables, drawn in brush and ink, contain scenes calculated to outrage horses.

Soho Square Mario Cavalli (1992, 11 min)
Hot time, summer in the city… A hued thought in a green shade – the life of a square from flesh to 'paint' via video. 24 hours of light.

Biogenesis William Latham (1993, 5 min)
Biogenesis shows the evolution of artificial life forms in a synthetic universe where 'survival of the fittest' is replaced by 'survival of the most aesthetic'. We see cellular evolution and the replication of mutations forming chain-like structures resembling coral.

What She Wants Ruth Lingford (1994, 5 min)
A woman travelling on the underground is bedevilled with images of desire. *What She Wants* – wholly created on an Amiga 1500 home computer – is a film about sex and shopping, the social deployment of sexuality, and capitalism in detumesence.

Feeling My Way Jonathan Hodgson (1997, 6 min)
An account of a journey from home to work as seen through the filter of the conscious and subconscious mind. Through the use of moving collages and painterly animation laid over Hi-8 footage, the viewer is able to share the traveller's experiences and his mental reactions to the trials and triviality of urban existence.

Withdrawal George Barber (1997, 4 min)
In the countryside, on a sunny day a family group repeatedly walk towards the camera. The 'home-movie' is looped and the footage is digitally manipulated so that each time they pass, the family members steadily disappear, the landscape also appearing to 'withdraw'.

Ferment Tim Macmillan (1999, 5 min)
In a quiet city square an old man clutches his chest and falls to the ground, and time stands still. We travel from the square, down streets, through buildings – the human condition unfolds in glimpses of frozen moments.

Love is All Oliver Harrison (1999, 3 min)
Winter bound, a snow queen dreams of love and the blooming of spring. Through frosted rococo cartouches she sings about the virtues of true love accompanied by miniature animated sequences.

Rotting Artist Ann Course & Paul Clark (2002, 3 min)
People try it on in the Croxley bunkers, and when the head of the household shoves his bendy cane brush right up the chimney we would do well to run to the other side of the road and watch it appear out the top for the lucky sight of it.

Perpetual Motion in the Land of Milk and Honey AL + AL (2004, 6 min)
AL + AL's grandfather James Brown is a retired engineer and inventor living in the north of England. The film re-fabricates his lifelong endeavours to break the law of physics and create a perpetual motion device. Free power for the people will produce a land flowing with milk and honey.

Synopses reproduced from www.animateonline.org

DVD/ PAL / Region 0

© The individual artists and LUX

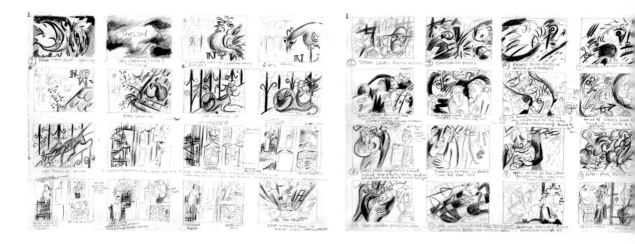

The animate! Book
Edited by Benjamin Cook and Gary Thomas

Published in Great Britain 2006 by
LUX, 3rd Floor, 18 Shacklewell Lane, London, UK
www.lux.org.uk
in association with Arts Council England
www.artscouncil.org.uk

Book production editor Eileen Daly
Design Joanna Deans at Identity
Printed by Die Keure, Belgium

Special thanks to Dick Arnall

ISBN 0 954 85692 9

A catalogue record for this book is available from the British Library

blue screen pantone: 2735, font: Avenir, stock: Chromomatt 170gsm

   animate!

158/*Stressed* Karen Kelly (1994)